D0939413

FASHION
INDIA

Thames & Hudson

Phyllida Jay

FASHION INDIA

Fashion India © 2015 Phyllida Jay

All Rights Reserved. No part of this publication may be reproduced or transmitted in any form or by any means, electronic or mechanical, including photocopy, recording or any other information storage and retrieval system, without prior permission in writing from the publisher.

First published in 2016 in paperback in the United States of America by Thames & Hudson Inc., 500 Fifth Avenue, New York, New York 10110

thamesandhudsonusa.com

Library of Congress Catalog Card Number 2015941296

ISBN 978-0-500-29201-3

Designed by Maggi Smith

Printed and bound in China by C & C Offset Printing Co. Ltd

page 1
Benares brocade sari,
Abraham and Thakore for Ekaya,
Autumn/Winter 2013.

page 2, left
Payal Khandwala,
figurative painting, 2007.
right
Payal Khandwala,'A Fine Balance',
Autumn/Winter 2013, Lakmé Fashion
Week, Mumbai.

page 3, left
Payal Khandwala,
abstract painting, oil on canvas, 2010.
middle
Payal Khandwala, oil on canvas, 2011.
right
Payal Khandwala,'A Fine Balance',
Autumn/Winter 2013.

page 6
Abu Jani & Sandeep Khosla, tulle coat
dress in three-dimensional mirror
embroidery with lotus motifs, Couture
2010.

Contents

Introduction

opposite
Rahul Mishra with
singer-actress Shruti
wearing his designs:
a silk jacket from 'Keep
it Simple and Sport',
Spring/Summer 2014
paired with a diamond-
motif Chanderi sari.
Photograph: R. Burman;
stylist: Mohit Rai for
*Harper's Bazaar Bride
India*, May 2014.

With India's flourishing economy, images of its malls, IT-orientated service sector, booming real estate, burgeoning consumer market and multi-billion-dollar film industry permeate the media. Yet equally India's image inheres in the ancient and the mythic, in gods and goddesses, religious custom and time-honoured traditions. Interestingly, both images – that of the ultra modern and of unchanging tradition – are actively nurtured to support the idea of an identity, culture and aesthetics intrinsic to Indian society. 'Paradox' has become the eternal buzz-word for India, as a land of seemingly irreconcilable, yet co-existing contrasts.

Among all of these manifestations of modern India, fashion has taken its place as a key mediator of both tradition and modernity. Yet Indian fashion's representation in the international media has so often relapsed into the cliches of Bollywood glitz and bridal wear that many will be unaware of the sheer diversity of Indian fashion and the very particular challenges that designers negotiate in this thriving non-Western industry.

A key shift in global opinion occurred when Rahul Mishra won the prestigious International Woolmark Prize in 2014. Global media coverage of Mishra's win expounded how it represented a milestone for the international image of Indian fashion. Many international fashion editors found themselves caught off-guard by the diversity of Indian fashion that Mishra's designs pointed towards.

This surprising diversity, often overlooked, holds the key to some of the most fascinating questions defining the Indian fashion industry today: namely, how and in what direction will Indian fashion grow? What is the future of traditional garments, such as the sari, now that young Indian women (and their mothers) increasingly turn towards the tunic and trouser combinations of the *salwar kameez* or *kurta churidar*, jeans or so-called Western-style clothing for everyday wear? What role will India's rich heritage of craft tradition play in the evolving identity of Indian fashion? Should Indian designers downplay traditional Indian silhouettes and ornamentation to aim commercially at the Western market? Or should they instead look inwards and cater to the home market for 'intrinsically Indian' clothing? And does sustained commercial success in Indian fashion imply only ever producing lavish ensembles for the all-important bridal market?

opposite
Actress Lisa Haydon in
a Tarun Tahiliani
bustier embellished
with Swarovski crystals,
worn with a tulle sari
decorated with tiny
floating flowers and
a hand-embroidered
threadwork border.

overleaf
J. J. Valaya's catwalk
finale for 'The Maharaja
of Madrid', India
Bridal Fashion Week,
Mumbai, 2013.

This raises the question of what exactly defines 'Indian' fashion in a country so diverse and fast-changing, with such a long history of sartorial fusion. Not least, what of the importance of oil-rich Persian Gulf countries as key consumer markets for many Indian designers – how will these markets grow and influence the trajectory of Indian fashion design? Furthermore, what role will India play in defining a pan-Asian movement of fashion, now that Asian countries rank among some of the most lucrative emerging markets for international luxury brands?

Another question all of this raises is what exactly is the relationship of Indian ethnic wear to Western fashion? It is common to make a sharp distinction between the two, attributing ethnic wear to unchanging dress and Western wear as part and parcel of a globalization-driven modernity. In *Dress and Ethnicity: Change Across Space and Time* (1995), Joanne Eicher argues that chiefly because a historical perspective in relation to Western dress is well established, in stark contrast to the dearth of dress histories of the non-Western world, non-Western dress is perceived to have undergone little change. In *Re-orienting Fashion: the Globalization of Asian Dress* (2003), Sandra Niessen writes that categorization of dress as either 'changing fashion' or 'unchanging tradition' is not only used to preserve boundaries between the West and non-West, but also serves as an important form of differentiation in non-Western countries as part of the ongoing dynamics of post-coloniality and globalization. In this sense, fashion produces tradition as much as it produces modernity. It is quite obvious, looking at the designers in this book, that ethnic dress is a dynamic form of fashion in its own right, subject to fluctuations in trends, creative appropriation and exotic imaginings tied up in notions of authenticity and Indian identity. This constant diagloue between tradition and modernity is a theme that underpins the work of many of the designers included in this book.

One of the key issues in Indian fashion is the dynamic between traditional ethnic and Western wear. Designers either stake out the terms of their design in an adherence to one or the other, or borrow from both in sophisticated dialogues that marry traditional hand-loom textiles with sharply tailored cuts or high-tech lycra with sari drapes, or reinvent *dhotis* as luxury evening wear. A further

point is raised by Eicher in *Dress and Ethnicity: Change Across Space and Time* (1995) when she asks, why, when Western wear is worn across the world, do we still call it by that name? Surely, she argues, it should be called something different such as cosmopolitan or world dress.

Another challenge Indian designers must often contend with, especially where their design practice centres around traditional hand-woven textiles or decorative embroidery, is the question of ethics, and how to work with India's craftworkers. While labour ethics along the supply chain are important in any aspect of the Indian fashion industry, including the workers who tailor mass ready-to-wear, it is in the sphere of designer fashion that labour used to produce hand-loom and craft becomes highlighted as part of a complex matrix of ethics, commerce, luxury, heritage and tradition. We will also see in the work of many designers the use of the symbolic textile *khadi* (hand-spun and/or woven cloth), which was at the centre of Mahatma Gandhi's movement for Swaraj (self-rule). Designers' use of *khadi* highlights the political nature of contemporary Indian fashion, where passionate views on home-grown luxury and intangible culture heritage represented in the materiality of hand-crafted textiles are tied up in a sense of pride and identity in being Indian in an emerging superpower. However, even as India forges ahead with space missions to Mars and building a cutting-edge technological service sector, its 'soft power' is closely bound up in ancient traditions of handmade crafts – one of the many paradoxes that are shaped and defined by the unevenness of India's development, as much as by its rich heritage of decorative arts and crafts. Many designers consciously place themselves at the front line of this Rubicon between the old and new, the rural and urban, analogue and digital worlds, and work with craftspeople to try to bridge the divide between India's craftworkers and the urban markets.

By bringing together a broad selection of designers in this book, what emerges is the way that Indian fashion both expresses and proposes ways of being Indian through a diverse array of design innovations. We also see the inherently ludic quality of Indian fashion design, which constantly mixes various stylistic forms as part of a much longer history of cultural exchange, assimilation and appropriation. Crossing boundaries of time and space, the

opposite
'Little Rabbit Ears' headpiece from Little Shilpa's presentation 'Disco Denimals', London Fashion Week, Spring/Summer 2015.

opposite
Manish Arora, black-
and-white butterfly
wing sequins create
a dégradé effect on
a dress with a ruff of
feathers at the neckline,
ready-to-wear,
Paris Fashion Week,
Spring 2012.

aesthetics of Indian fashion manifest the changing socio-economic and cultural worlds of its consumers, whether in the mesmerizing, opulent and jewel-encrusted aesthetic surfaces of bridal wear, minimal hand-loom fashioned into leopard-print saris or elegant suits, the deconstructed sari drapes that form glamorous cocktail wear or the fusing of ethnic garments with Western traditions of cut and construction, so that eventually an entirely new kind of fashion is born.

It is the very diversity of Indian designers, how each responds in very different ways to the dynamic between Indian and Western fashion, their ability to harness India's rich textile traditions in ingenious fabrication, or the way different designers combine contemporary Western silhouettes with traditional embroidery techniques that makes Indian fashion a never-ending spectrum of complex permutations between the old and the new; the minimal and lavishly ornamented; the traditional and the cutting edge.

A 1997 study on the French luxury fashion industry by sociologist Diana Crane assists in understanding the scope of designers included in this book. Crane defined high-end fashion as that where its value is derived from association with an individual whose creativity and vision is perceived as uniquely embodied in the design. In turn, these designers will be members of the Paris-based fashion industry body The Fédération Française de la Couture, du Prêt-à-Porter des Couturiers et des Créateurs de Mode. In his 2009 book *Ramp Up*, journalist and author Hindol Sengupta revealed that the Fashion Design Council of India (FDCI), established in 1999, was based partly on the French model. Members of the FDCI (over 350 in all) may be involved in the creation of couture or ready-to-wear, with the FDCI officially stipulating that membership is based on a designer possessing a 'Signature style...unique and identifiable'. Most of the designers included in this book are FDCI members, and all are recognized for their creative talent and unique contribution to the developing identity of contemporary Indian fashion.

Bollywood:
luxury bridal and formal wear

opposite
Tarun Tahiliani, ivory
net *lehenga* (left) with
multi-coloured *resham*
embroidery and a
broad *gota* appliqué
band. An ensemble
in fuchsia silk dupion,
brocade georgette and
soft net (right) hand
embroidered with
gold *zardosi*.

below
Vidya Balan in
Sabyasachi on
the cover of *Marie
Claire*, October 2009.
Photograph: Avinash
Gowariker.

Lavish ornamentation, exotic imagery and regal styling that recall the royal courts of Indian history: these are just some of the themes in the collections produced by the designers featured in this chapter. Only the wealthiest can afford to buy their couture and luxury prêt-à-porter, but their influence spreads far and wide through their Bollywood costumes and the film stars and industrialists who wear their clothes at weddings, parties and press launches (also fuelling a rampant market for designer copies in India).

In India, religious festivals and family occasions are celebrated on a regular basis. The ethnic formal wear worn is an important focus for Indian designers along with the all-important bridal market. Indian weddings are organized around an astrological calendar of auspicious and inauspicious days mainly between October and February. Christiane Brosius, Professor of Visual and Media Anthropology at Heidelberg University, has researched and written extensively on the Indian middle class and consumer growth, calling the wedding market a sphere of consumption that highlights the creative potential of commodities. With changing work cultures and lifestyles, she explains, organizing the wedding increasingly shifts from the domain of the bride and groom's families to non-religious specialists offering a 'total wedding package'.

The wedding can be seen as a microcosm of the economic and social changes in India since the early 1990s. In this sense, weddings take on a new significance as a form of display and social cohesion, tied up in both local and global aesthetics of conspicuous consumption, luxury and class status. As Brosius argues, what is new in the big fat Indian wedding of the post-millennium is the celebration of class status and the scale of pomp and display.[1]

Apocryphal stories circulate of weddings involving hundreds of guests,

above   Raghavendra Rathore dressing actor Anil
Kapoor backstage at the India Bridal Fashion Week,
Delhi, 2013.

right   Maharaja of Jodhpur Sardar Singh ji,
Raghavendra Rathore's great-grandfather.

multiple venues across international locations and unlimited spending. The
wedding for the niece of steel tycoon Lakshmi Mittal is rumoured to have cost
sixty million euros, with nuptials relocating hundreds of guests to Barcelona
where the National Museum of Catalan Art was closed to the public on the day
the celebrations took place. But even for families with less stratospheric budgets,
the wedding remains an important family, social and cultural event on which
a large amount of money in proportion to earnings is spent. Across Indian towns
and cities wedding season brings a daily routine of snarled traffic as bridal
processions with grooms on horseback and brass bands parade the streets. As
many as thirty thousand weddings take place in Delhi alone on one of the most
astrologically auspicious days.

The designers explored in this chapter offer a regal and aristocratic vision
of luxury and bridal fashion that draws on the opulence of Mughal and Rajput
royal history in the north and the Deccani courts of the south. This mythic
and historical retelling of India resonates with a new mood of optimism and
cultural pride engendered by economic growth and India's increasing presence
on the world stage. Perhaps this is best summed up by a statement made by
J. J. Valaya:

*We are the new Royalty...a new Indian Raj that is determined to spread its wings
globally. Our evolving look is a curious signature, a fusion that has found widespread acceptance...because of its inspiring balance between our rich past and
our elegantly mad, yet glorious, future.*

This ambitious, visionary sense of fashion's role in defining India's future has much deeper roots in the way the Indian fashion industry emerged. The immediate post-independence era in India was defined by the social-ist policies of Jawaharlal Nehru, the first prime minister. This resulted in strict regulations and high taxes on imported goods, little or no access to credit for the large majority of India's population and a pervasive attitude to consump-tion grounded in saving and thrift. The retail market was dominated by small family-owned businesses or home-grown pan-Indian brands created by the great industrialist families such as the Tatas and Birlas. Ready-to-wear clothing was almost non-existent and people bought fabric to take to local tailors. Foreign goods were hard to obtain and expensive due to high import taxes. Access to foreign brands usually meant having a relative living or travelling abroad who could send back gifts of coveted Western brands. Yet in contrast to this general mood of austerity, the Bollywood films, which became such a unifying marker of shared Indian experience and identity in the post-colonial era, depicted wealth and success with lavish modern settings where electric goods such as air-conditioners or telephones and Western-style clothing symbolized modernity and the consumer-good life.

right
J. J. Valaya takes a bow with actress Kangana Ranaut for his 'Azrak' collection, Wills Lifestyle India Fashion Week, 2012.

opposite
Model Rachel Bayros wears
a richly embroidered kalidar,
India Bridal Fashion Week,
Mumbai, 2013.

below
Embroidered 24 *kalis* (panels)
anarkali, illustration J. J. Valaya.

J. J. Valaya

By the late 1980s the changing political and economic structure of India meant a gradual loosening of its tight regulatory policies on foreign direct investment and imports. It was in this broader climate that many of the designers featured in this chapter began their careers, either through informal training assisting Bollywood costume designers, or as attendees of the newly launched National Institute of Fashion Technology (NIFT) in Delhi, the first educational institution in India to offer courses aimed at fashion as a career. Delhi-based designer J. J. Valaya began his career at this time when there were no fashion weeks in India, no fashion press and a limited consumer base. His childhood was spent travelling from place to place due to his father's career in the Indian army.

My story began in 1988. When interning as a chartered accountant in Chandigarh, I realized that I was miserable doing what I was doing and had to make a drastic career change. In fact, the only bright spot was in my imagination, when I would dream about the decor of my office (when I would have one) at the accountancy... Then I discovered the National Institute of Fashion Technology in 1989, which was a brand new institute being run out of a makeshift campus in New Delhi.

Valaya describes what it was like to be a young designer starting out in the late 1980s at the very inception of the Indian fashion industry.

It was quite amazing actually. Simply because we had no benchmarks to follow, no mistakes to learn from, and so we had to make ours to become wiser. Coming from a time when there were no TV channels in India (other than the national channel Doordarshan which primarily focused on rural farmers), no magazines covering fashion let alone being fully dedicated to it, no newspaper supplements writing about fashion, no retail outlets other than two newly opened ones (in Mumbai and Bangalore), no fashion weeks (the first one happened in 1999 after some of us collectively created the Fashion Design Council of India), no internet, very limited customers in general (as the concept of expensive clothes off the rack was alien to India). Compare that to now, when everything has changed and fashion and style in general in India are in overdrive! Let's just say, we were fortunate to have been there when it all began.

At that time designer clothing was a difficult proposition in India. Just as

opposite
She wears a lamé
lehenga and bustier,
he wears a woven and
embroidered metallic
jacquard flared
sherwani. Photograph:
J. J. Valaya, shot on
location at The Lodhi
Hotel, Delhi. Courtesy
Harper's Bazaar India,
May 2009.

below
Keyhole detail on an
anarkali.

*My mind and spirit travel to wherever I find history,
culture and contradiction. Evolving with global trends
and re-creating traditional designs with modern twists
is important.*

below
Model Ninja Singh
wears Valaya's
bridal collection,
2011.

we read recent history of Western fashion as being centred around the development of European couture and the luxury fashion brand from the point at which in the 1850s Charles Frederick Worth first sewed labels with his name into the nape of his designs, so we need to understand how the idea of the 'designer' developed in India and the broader economic, social and cultural conditions that facilitated this.[2] Mukti Khaire, a professor at Harvard, has analysed the emergence of opulent bridal and ethnic formal wear inspired by royal costume as a response to the evolving context of designer fashion in the domestic market. Personal tailors (many of which can be found across towns and cities in India) are commonly how clothing is acquired. Khaire found that at first it was difficult for designers to persuade customers of the value of their designs; the question of conceptualization, cut and design input was subsumed to the idea that designers were 'just' like

tailors. Khaire argues that in response there evolved the aesthetic of densely embroidered and ornamented clothing where the value was evident in the technical skill and the quantity of labour involved. This enabled designers to carve out a unique identity as arbiters of taste and luxury. Valaya himself reflects on his development as a designer.

From an all-ivory Western graduation collection at NIFT, devoid of any embellishments, to understanding quite early...that Indians considered weddings as key events in their lives and so deciding to focus on trousseaux and wedding-related apparel was another learning curve.

Forty per cent of Valaya's business comes from menswear, which is one of the strongest luxury markets in India. He also designs for West Asian royalty and is planning to develop an online business for the growing consumer market driven by youth day wear. As the market for luxury formal and bridal wear has grown, so the tastes of consumers have shifted.

Until a few years ago, the heavier the outfit in terms of weight and the more the embroidery and embellishments, the more exquisite and expensive the outfit was considered to be. Today, whilst the look and feel still has to be heavy, albeit with finer embellishments, there is an equal focus on cut, styles, fabric and the eventual weight. The client today versus the client twenty years back are two different beings. With the internet shrinking the world and our clients being well travelled, well heeled, well read, we have confident individuals who know their minds, respect their culture and have embraced modernity with a sophisticated vengeance.

Often, in terms of global fashion, influence seems to flow one way, so, for example, many European fashion designers constantly reference and source from India. Valaya's work represents an opposite direction to this flow, and as

below Fantasy worlds of the maharajas are a common theme among Indian bridal designers. Photograph: J. J. Valaya.

bottom Actor Rahul Dev in a white *sherwani* with embroidery over black appliqué. Photograph: J. J. Valaya.

above
'The Maharaja of Madrid'
menswear collection, 2013.

Royals and nomads have always been the base for all my designs; I don't know whether the fact that I was born in Jodhpur, Rajasthan, known equally for its maharajas and for its nomads, had anything to do with it.

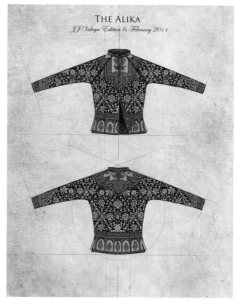

below and opposite
Alika jackets are a signature
classic of the Valaya brand and
are reworked each season.

THE ALIKA

J J Valaya Edition 6, February 2011

above
On a set inspired
by royal palaces,
model Noyonika
Chatterjee walks
for J. J. Valaya at
PCJ Delhi Couture
Week, 2012.

well as drawing from the archives of India's royal history, he also looks to global cultural references. For example, his 2013 'The Maharaja of Madrid' collection took inspiration from Spanish dance and architecture.

I have always believed that the old and the new must and can co-exist. Therefore, my mind and spirit travel to wherever I find history, culture and contradiction. Evolving with global trends and re-creating traditional designs with modern twists is important.

Like many of the established bridal designers, Valaya has a keen sense of building his brand along the lines of the French luxury house with diffusion lines and aesthetic codes that define the house style. Valaya's Alika jacket is one such example, designed, he says, to be a classic in the same way as 'the Gucci loafer, the Burberry trench coat, the Hermes bag or the Chanel tweed jacket'. Based in part on the traditional *sadri*, the Alika jacket is reinterpreted each season while retaining its defining features. Another aspect of this 'code' building is the Diasun, a pattern made from interlocking Vs representing the Valaya name as well as motifs from the brand's crest logo. This recognizable pattern is printed on the linings of all Valaya couture and prêt pieces and is an attempt to deal with the problem of plagiarism in India. It is protected by a copyright patent.

opposite
A bridal *lehenga* embellished with
Swarovski crystals and shaded
velvet appliqué in a paisley design
on a thread-embroidered brocade
base, paired with a contoured *kurti*,
embroidered *dupatta* and veil.

Tarun Tahiliani

below
Model in an outfit
from the 'With Love
From Taj' collection,
Taj Mahal, Agra.
It was part
of a project
commissioned by
the Taj Mahotsav
Committee
(Uttar Pradesh
Tourism).
Photograph:
Pravin Talan.

India's first multi-designer boutique, in 1987. In 1991 he returned to the United States to study at the Fashion Institute of Technology, New York (while he was away his sister Tina managed Ensemble). On returning to India for the second time he launched his eponymous design label.

I am an Indian who was brought up with a strong English influence and live by the mantra – India Modern. I grew up in Bombay, in a post-colonial, socialist India, where the elite clung to Jesuit schools and piano lessons and the craft of India shrivelled up from a lack of design innovation and proper patronage. Slowly, a new philosophy began to develop out of this bleak environment: one that was awakened to India's truly great heritage and one that understood that contemporary design could give India's rich traditions a new voice and thus, a new resonance.

Fashion colleges were not established in India until the late 1980s, so many of the older generation of Indian designers began their career designing film costume for Bollywood. Tarun Tahiliani took a different route altogether, gaining a degree in business management from the Wharton School of Business, Pennsylvania. When he returned to India he saw the huge potential of the nascent luxury fashion market and, with his wife Sal, opened 'Ensemble',

The Tahilianis opened Ensemble at a time where there was no fashion media or fashion weeks in India.

When we started Ensemble in 1987, I felt the time was right because of an India Today article that talked of a nascent fashion movement via

right
Gold brocade *sherwani* embroidered with *zardosi* and *gota*, paired with crinkled *kurta* and contrasting *churidars*. A pearl and metal string with a jewelled brooch is typical of styling that evokes Mughal splendour.

far right
Ivory gold *sherwani* with satin quilt appliqué and *gota* embroidery.

opposite
Zardosi embroidered *sherwani* with aubergine *kurta*, *churidar* and a brocade pre-pleated stole (left). Red kimkhab brocade *sherwani* with draped *kamarbandh* (right).

a few new boutiques in Delhi. It was a risk, there was no fashion, it was a culture of exhibitions cum sale. People tried things on over their clothes in little art galleries that doubled as retail spaces by people who came in...It was a very exciting venture to embark upon because it felt full of possibilities and we were backed by the family business who owned the space. It really was not as much of a risk as if we had just ventured out to start a store from scratch. I daresay that it would never have happened now that you ask me the question, it would actually have happened only in the circumstances that we had.

The Tahilianis co-founded Ensemble with the late Rohit Khosla. He remains a beacon within Indian fashion, instrumental to its early formation and identity.

Khosla went and studied and worked with Versace. At the time we met him he had just moved back from working with Albert Nipon

in New York and was really the only person who had exposure to international fashion and luxury brands and how they were structured. It's not only that we learned that from him, but even just how things should be presented, the idea of collections, what was cohesive and what the fashion world abroad stood for. It was Rohit Khosla who taught us the principles of fashion, styling and boutiques; he took us across stores in London and New York, said what worked and what didn't and slowly evolved our own modern Indian formula of what we wanted to do with the resources that were available to us.

Tahiliani often speaks of the 'colonial mindset' of his and previous generations, where the West has been something aspired to – as something to emulate. With economic growth there has been an explosion of the consumption of foreign brands in India as well as a counter movement in the form of traditional Indian craft interpreted for bridal and ethnic formal wear.

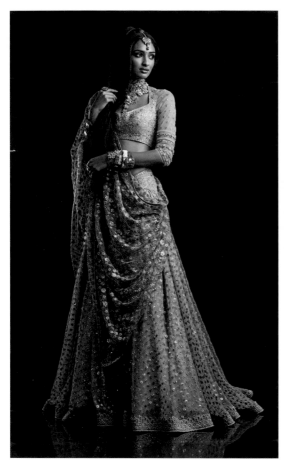

above left
Gold tulle *lehenga*
and *dupatta*.
Choli and hip yoke
embellished with
Swarovski crystals.

above right
Yellow and orange
silk georgette
lehenga with
gota and *resham*
embroidery.

*India is the embroidery capital of the world...
I combined this aspect with ready-to-wear
techniques of pattern and fit. I started the store
with my wife to promote the best of Indian design
because I thought it odd that forty years after
independence we were still sending our best
products abroad.*

A large part of the revival of embellishment
techniques, notably ornate *zardosi*,
chikankari and *resham* embroidery by

designers such as Tahiliani, has been to
forge a language of luxury, an invented
tradition that resonates with the growing
affluence and the idea of a search for one's
'roots'. Tahiliani's 2014 couture exposition,
'The Modern Mughals', was inspired by
the dress of Mughal emperors and the
nawabs and begums who ruled the semi-
autonomous princely states under Mughal
rule. The collection included keyhole
jackets paired with *lehengas* for the bride

above
Wedding *lehenga*
ensembles, couture
collection, 2010.

and men's *sherwanis*, currently a widely popular silhouette for the groom. The years of economic opportunity after the long period of socialism proved a watershed for consumption. As the middle class grew and levels of wealth increased, so a culture of conspicuous consumption developed around weddings, traditionally events at which families placed great importance on festivities. Since 1991 the Indian wedding has taken on a new character altogether.

It is perhaps no surprise that as people looked to express status and wealth the past splendour of Mughal royalty was fixed in the collective imagination as the ultimate fantasy of luxury; a fantasy propagated since the birth of the Indian nation in Hindi-language cinemas with films such as *Humayan* (1945) cementing the nostalgic vision of Mughal splendour in popular culture. More recent such films have included *Umrao Jaan* (1981) as well as

opposite
The traditional sari drape melds with cut and construction techniques, 'Kumbhback', Autumn/Winter 2013.

above left and above centre
For Autumn/Winter 2013, drapes and an orange colour palette were inspired by a trip to the Kumbh Mela, a mass Hindu pilgrimage in which over 100 million Hindus gather to bathe in the sacred River Ganges. Drape dress, 'Kumbhback', Autumn/Winter, 2013.

above right
Sadhu-inspired draped top with draped skirt, 'Kumbhback', Autumn/Winter 2013.

its remake in 2006 starring Aishwarya Rai and Abhishek Bachchan.

These representations of Mughal splendour have reinforced its popularity for bridal wear, with designers such as Tahiliani being coveted by the new consumer market for their nostalgic vision of royal luxury. Yet Tahiliani is also critical of the excesses of the bridal market, where bridal wear has often become associated with heavy, unwieldy pieces and an excess of ornamentation that overpowers a more design-focused approach. As ornate as his collections are, he has also worked in recent years to be innovative and use fabrics such as tulle to make lighter, more fluid bridal wear.

Indian fashion today now understands Western principles of cut and construct, fit and finish and we understand that as an Indian couture house we need to be more accessible to changing demographics. When it comes to Indian couture there is a visible evolution. People get used to the fit and proportion of Western clothing so they start enjoying well-cut and fitted clothes which are easy to move around in. As most bridal wear revolves around couture there is no fun in heavy clothes which restrict movement and come in

the way of the wedding celebrations – hence the shift to lighter outfits is a key trend I have seen through the years. Over the last twenty years, I have seen dupattas being pared down in weight and size. In terms of design nowadays, there are a few brides who are happy to be a little more experimental sometimes with what they wear for their sangeet or mehendi. When it comes to the wedding lehenga itself, most people like to stay with what is traditional though.

Tahiliani has developed several key retail strategies, including bridal couture costing between 11,500 to 60,000 USD, concept saris, prêt-à-porter ethnic wear as well as his less well-known work with Western silhouettes.

For Wills Lifestyle India Fashion Week (Autumn/Winter 2013) Tahiliani's 'Kumbhback' collection was inspired by his visit to the Maha Kumbh Mela, held every three years, and one of the largest religious gatherings on earth with as many as one hundred million pilgrims travelling to bathe in the River Ganges. Inspired by sadhus and pilgrims, he created a collection of saffron, maroon, red, blue, rust and amber drapes, evoking the unique aesthetics of this religious occasion.

Abu Jani &
Sandeep Khosla

With the work of Mumbai-based designers Abu Jani and Sandeep Khosla we can understand the idea of couture translated from the French into the local context of India. Famous for their ornate bridal trousseaux and ethnic formal wear, yet accessible only to the elite few, they represent all that is the pinnacle of the idea of bespoke luxury fashion in India today. Jani and Khosla had an instant rapport when they met at a mutual friend's launch in 1986 and have worked together on both fashion and interior design for over 25 years. In 2013 they celebrated this milestone in their two-volume book *India Fantastique* with text by art critic Gayatri Sinha, a choice they made because:

We wanted a narrative that would go beyond the narrow parameters of a fashion biography and see our work in design from a wider perspective.

below
Shweta Bachchan Nanda in a heavily ornamented *lehenga* where each of the *kalis* displays a different embroidery pattern.

'Couture' is a word that inspires awe, but it is an entirely Euro-centric vision of the relationship between design, luxury and the highly skilled crafts that define the idea of bespoke 'couture'. The word 'couture' has become an over-used and misunderstood term in the wake of rapid expansion of European luxury brands and practices that are more akin to customized rather than bespoke clothing.[3] Not least, forms of bespoke production constitute an important aspect of the fashion markets in non-Western fashion centres, making it imperative to understand 'couture' practices in local contexts.

The book launch was a glittering party (held at the 'world's first billion-dollar home', Antilla, which was built by industrialist Mukesh Ambani) attended by the prominent Bachchan family and a host of Bollywood stars. Jani and Khosla embody the meaning of 'couture' in their social milieu and elite patronage within the Indian luxury market. It is reported that they closely vet prospective bridal customers, and 'personally meet a client only if her wedding *lehenga* budget exceeds Rs 10 lakh!'.[4] They once hosted a television series for NDTV called *First Ladies*, in which they interviewed the wives of leading Bollywood stars and businessmen; these women were also their personal customers and friends.

We have always been the odd ones out when it comes to standard fashion practices. We rarely do fashion shows nor do we advertise in a big way. We prefer to let our clothes do the talking. We began with no formal training and a paltry financial investment.... We began with couture and couture remains our calling.

above
Metres of gold tissue
ruched using
embroidery stitches
form the body of this
long flared coat.

The brand evolved through word of mouth. We never allowed financial, creative or market constraints to colour or compromise our creativity. It wasn't economically prudent to do this but it has paid off creatively. Our design aesthetic is maximalist. More is more. We believe in layering, sumptuous pure fabrics, the finest embroideries and the most intricate embellishments. There are no shortcuts when it comes to couture. There cannot be because the very nature of it calls for a meticulous and painstaking attention to detail. It's all about the nitpicking. Finishing is key and we refuse to compromise on the feel of a garment. Every outfit is a flight of fancy.

Their design signature is highly ornate bridal and formal ethic wear that draws on royal costume and fantasy and grandeur.

Royalty and India are inseparable, both in the imagination of the Western eye as well as in the collective soul and memory of the Indian. The Maharaja look is a natural result of wanting to replicate the grandeur and majesty of that world. And nothing calls for regal like a wedding. That it became a fashion trend is therefore no surprise.

When steel tycoon Lakshmi Mittal's only daughter, Vanisha, got married in 2004 she wore a red and gold Jani and Khosla *lehenga*. Her wedding to banker Amit Bhatia took place at the Palace of Versailles in France. When Hyderabad-based industrialist GVK Reddy's granddaughter married, it was one of the most lavish weddings ever seen in South India, with Indian media reporting on the

opposite
Bridal *lehenga*
heavily embroidered
in traditional gold
and silver *gota*
embroidery.

right
Gold dress hand-
embroidered
with pieces of
metal inspired
by South Indian
gold jewelry.

as a 'natural' consumer and producer of luxury in its own right. As couture designers to film stars and India's wealthiest businessmen, Jani and Khosla are at the cutting edge of this new era of redux and resurgence.

Fine craftsmanship is an ancient craft in our country. Indians have been connoisseurs and consumers of luxury for centuries. Our appreciation of lavish embroideries and embellishments is wired into our DNA. The 70s and early 80s witnessed a dilution in the quality of techniques. As designers we saw it as our mission to restore these crafts to their former glory and then reinterpret them through our creations.

As one of India's longest-established couturiers, they are well aware of the contradiction between a lack of international profile for many Indian designers and yet the inspiration, in terms of Indian culture and its highly skilled craftspeople, that European fashion has consistently drawn upon. For example, Chanel's Paris-Bombay collection in 2011, Prada's use of *chikankari* embroidery in its 2012 resort wear and Isabel Marant's Gujarati mirrorwork jackets for H&M in 2013.

Whilst Indian design houses are still to make a significant mark in the international arena, the influence of India is writ large in global haute couture. From our silhouettes to embroideries and embellishments, every major designer has been influenced by India and incorporated this influence in their collections.

This is a highly sensitive and important issue in terms of the politics of non-Western fashion: Western designers have often translated inspiration from 'exotic' places into fashion, but those 'exotic' places are not seen as sources of design ideation in their own right. This indicates a highly political sense of what it means to be a designer in today's India. Indian and

venue with wedding decor designed by Jani and Khosla.

Anthropologist Christiane Brosius has written about the pleasure spaces and levels of consumption that have emerged since the 1990s, analysing the Indian real estate and tourism industries that produce the 'seemingly contradictory rhetoric of modernity paired with the nostalgic vision of royal grandeur and patriotism'.[5] If India's image internationally has often been a stereotypical one of poverty and overpopulation, this new rhetoric of a proud modernity produced by aesthetics of grandeur and centred on corporate leaders as the new royalty has sought to counter that image. The highly political nature of fashion and its role in mediating images of Indian identity both on the domestic and international stage has been revealed. A new rhetoric of Indian luxury has also been produced, only heightened by the acceleration of European luxury brands into India. A discourse has emerged that has staked out India

Our design aesthetic is maximalist, more is more.

formal fashion education did not exist in India. As veterans of the fashion industry they know the challenges facing young designers and the development necessary to the industry as a whole.

We need public sector funding which will enable us to ramp up infrastructure and create training, R&D and educational facilities. We need trained pattern cutters, machinery, and state-of-the-art factories in order to achieve economies of scale and perfect our product. India has no dearth of talent; what we lack is investors willing to take Indian labels, nurture them on a creative and financial level and market them on a national and global level... We also need to use institutions like FDCI to work cohesively as a single lobby to advocate for our 'cause' and become a strong presence on the world stage.

above
A contemporary interpretation of white-on-white Chikankari embroidery.

opposite
Actress Sonali Bendre in mirrorwork *anarkali*.

Western designers alike often invest their conceptual process with similar creative appropriations of an imagined, exotic India, which reflects a complicated history of Orientalism, which has both served and defined the West by default of its exotic other; or more recently Indian designers have harnessed these exoticisms in the service of the growing heritage industry for consumption by Indian elites.

Like many of the designers who began their careers in the 1980s, Jani and Khosla had no formal training. They both worked for Bollywood costume designer Xerxes Bhathena, a typical route into design when

For *India Fantastique* they used international models and locations to show how their designs can be worn by anyone, anywhere.

We will only be able to break free of stereotypes when we are able to position ourselves correctly. This requires capital. We need to be visible, whether it is establishing boutiques, advertising, or PR. A fabulous product is a given but it is only the beginning. Fashion is aspirational. One needs to build that aspiration along with awareness. For many years India has been seen as a producer of mass-market, high-street style garments. It now needs to be recognized as a creator of high fashion couture too.

opposite
Silk brocade *achkan* paired with
silk *dhoti* with sash in gold tissue, BMW
India Bridal Fashion Week, Delhi, 2014.

Raghavendra Rathore

below left
Embroidered *kurta* waistcoat, BMW India Bridal Fashion Week, Delhi, 2013.

below right
Actress Dia Mirza is the 'show stopper' for Rathore at BMW India Bridal Fashion Week, Mumbai, 2013.

As a member of Jodhpur's royal family, designer Raghavendra Rathore's own life is intimately bound up in his vision of men's luxury fashion, one of the strongest markets in India. In particular, Rathore reinvents the dress of the maharajas originally seen in sepia images of erstwhile Rajput kings, forever suspended in a world of fantasy and luxury. They were equally at ease whether in full regalia, at the helm of their princely states, or dressed in the bespoke Savile Row suits they would have tailored on their sojourns to London.

Yet their relationship with the British was deeply ambiguous. As the colonial power, the British enabled them to rule through the uneasy truce of accepting them as princes but not kings. This is reflected in the legacy of their dress codes, which were a fusion of Indian and British influences.

The East India Company and the British had an undeniable influence on the attire of the maharajas during that time...the original Indian clothing was all about the unstitched draped cloth, mainly in pure fabrics such as cotton and silk, with the Mughals introducing stitched garments in the form of pants and the flowing angrakha. The British introduced more structure to the garments of royalty and a fusion emerged with structured but ornamental clothing.

Rathore's speciality is the *bandhgala*, a fitted, hip-length jacket. In common with the Nehru jacket (named after India's first prime minister in the 1940s), the *bandhgala* has a *band gale ka* (which is Hindi for a closed neck collar). The Nehru jacket was based on the longer *sherwani*, a fusion of the *salwar kameez* and British frock-coat in the era of Mughal rule and the East India Company. *Bandhgalas* are particularly associated with the maharajas who ruled the princely

A classic black bandhgala
jacket with breeches.
Nothing says 'modern royal'
better than this.

right
The Jodhpuri
bandhgala jacket
is a signature piece
of the Raghavendra
Rathore label.

states at the time of British rule. Rathore
describes his signature style as

A classic black bandhgala *jacket with breeches.*
Nothing says 'modern royal' better than this.

The *bandhgala* is often called 'the prince's
jacket' and is a staple silhouette for
politicians, dignitaries and businessmen
who wish to demonstrate their 'Indian-
ness' and patriotism. Before he returned
to India in 1994 to set up his own label,
Rathore studied at the Parsons School of
Design and spent his early career working
in New York.

At Donna Karan I learnt to build value in simpler
clothes for the upper section of the mass market
under the DKNY label and a completely different
experience was required at Oscar de la Renta,
as it is positioned in the uber luxury segment
of fashion.

His own work is informed by ideas of blue-
blooded good taste and the uniformity of
men's tailoring, with idiosyncratic twists
of individuality through tiny but all-
important details. These are codes that
must be imbibed and known, just as in the
arcane world of secrets and symbols that
defined the different Savile Row tailors in
London. According to Rathore, the Jodhpuri
bandhgala must fit like a glove; the hem

must end at the root of the thumb when
the arms are at the side of the body, the
armhole must be cut high and, when worn,
the top two buttons must be left undone.
It is best made from cashmere, wool, *khadi*
or silk, and worn with a pair of breeches,
blue denims for a smart–casual look or
flat-front, slim-cut trousers. Hand-woven
or mill-woven fabrics such as linen prove
the best in terms of structuring the garment
in the summer collection of waistcoats
and *kurtas*, while silk is the fabric of choice
when it comes to the winter collection and
the festive season.

Along with *bandhgala*, Rathore
designs Jodhpuri breeches associated
with polo and the aristocracy, as well
as womenswear, which often adapts
masculine silhouettes and tailoring as well
as more conventional ethnic womenswear.

top left and right
Jodhpuri *bandhgala* waistcoat with collar and pocket embroidery detailing paired with classic jodhpur breeches.

above
Rathore draws inspiration from historical images of the safari suit as well as polo matches.

right
Safari Collection: cotton waistcoat with bellows pocket and safari detailing worn with white cotton shirt and trousers in russet brown.

opposite
'India Modern', Winter/Festive 2014, Lakmé
Fashion Week, Mumbai. The collection
was conceptualized around a fictional
Jaipur bride. The term 'India Modern' is
a shorthand frequently used by Indian
designers to describe contemporization
of traditional craft and ethnic silhouettes.

Anita Dongre

below
Pink *lehenga* with
intricate *gota patti*
embroidery.

As this chapter demonstrates, although
bridal wear in general can be characterized
by opulence and the extensive use of
ornamentation, within that broad aesthetic
framework designers forge very different
interpretations and design signatures.
Mumbai-based Anita Dongre's bridal wear
is no exception. She offers *lehengas* and
bridal saris that are distinctive for their
light silks and simple colourways of gold
or white embroidery set against bright
jewel and pastel hues.

Her brands include AND (Western
wear), Global Desi (Indo-Western), Timeless
(bridal wear), Grassroots (eco-friendly) and
AD Menswear. A vegan and passionate
animal rights supporter, Dongre was also
an early adopter of India's fairtrade NGO
Shop for Change, using its organic cotton
in a range of branded lines. Bridal wear
forms one of her six diffusion brands, sold
both at her own chain of stores and at over
500 multi-brand outlets across India.

'Jaipur bride', 2013, took inspiration
from Dongre's family roots in Jaipur,
Rajasthan. *Gota patti* (appliqué using gold
ribbons) was used across a collection of
bridal wear that drew on Jaipur's royal
history and architecture for aesthetic
inspiration and styling of an atmospheric
lookbook and fashion film.

The goal of Dongre's ready-to-wear
offerings across her diffusion lines is
partly to cater to different body types,
and this is no less true of her bridal wear.
Although the perception of bridal wear
as traditional ethnic dress might foster
the view that it somehow elides fashion
and its trends, in fact designer bridal
wear continuously incorporates global
trends and body ideals into its aesthetics.
As a guest blog by Shinjini Amitabh
Chawla on e-commerce website Indian
Roots advised, whether a bride is
an 'apple', 'pear', 'strawberry', 'ruler'
or 'hourglass' shape, an appropriate
lehenga blouse combination can be
found. According to Chawla, the
lehenga can be 'full-ghera or fish-cut
with a short *choli* and net *dupatta*'; heavy
embroidery can be included on all or
certain parts of the *lehenga* to emphasize
or play down certain areas such as the
bust, hips or waist.[6] The localizing of
Western fashion trends also means
they fit with norms of modesty and
respectability.[7] The conjunction of global
trends incorporated into traditional ethnic
bridal wear provides the perfect balance
between tradition and modernity for
a bride on her wedding day. Magazines

left
Royal blue raw silk *lehenga* with intricate *gota patti* embroidery inspired by the architecture of Jantar Mantar (a Mughal-era equinoctial sundial built in the early 18th century). Styled with a raw silk *bandi* and embroidered net *dupatta*.

below
Burnt orange silk *achkan* paired with ivory *salwar*.

and increasingly blogs are crucial mediators of Western and local ideals of beauty and body shape, taking the role of intermediaries and providing guidance with the intimate tone of a friend on how best to style oneself according to these ideals. Designers also play a key role in guiding consumers through the complex demands of the wedding by providing them with context-appropriate fashion.[8] Comfort and practicality are an important part of Dongre's ready-to-wear bridal offering,

which is designed with very modern practicalities in mind.

A modern bride wants to dance, and enjoy herself...on her wedding day celebrations, she doesn't want to be weighed down by a lehenga *made unbearably heavy with weighty fabric and embroidery. I design bridal wear to be fluid and light so the bride can move freely.*

Vogue India described Dongre's 2013 bridal collection as where, 'The modern Indian

below
Blue raw silk *lehenga* embellished with *gota patti* and *zardosi*. Paired with a *resham bandi*.

right
White open-textured *sherwani* with gold hand embroidery around the neck, styled with white cotton *kurta* and lime green *ghera salwar*.

bride doesn't hide in her glass palace like a coy damsel…this bride is tech-savvy, loves her vino, even drives her own jeep.'[9]

As Brosius reflects, taste, class and cosmopolitan identity are signified by the ability to 'stage the world' in one event.[10] Clear in Dongre's vision is the new India, rich with the promise of its technology and service sector boom; the visual imagery of her campaign brings together tradition and modernity, providing guidance on how the consumer can position herself within these narratives of refinement, royal princesses, ancient traditions, global modernity and contemporary lifestyles. Each season Dongre draws on a fictitious muse Nayantara, who she says is

A young, effervescent girl who challenges convention, yet loves all things traditional. Coming from a royal lineage, Nayantara epitomizes modern-day femininity juxtaposed with a free-spirited, adventurous soul.

opposite
'The Age of Innocence', *Marie Claire*.
Stylist: Pearl Shah; location: a haveli,
Rajasthan; photograph: Aneev Rao
for *Marie Claire India*, October 2012.

Sabyasachi Mukherjee

below right
'Opium', PCJ Delhi
Couture Week,
2013, shows the
distinctive aesthetics
of Sabyasachi's
ethnic formal
wear displays

In the early millennium a new wave of bridal designers emerged. Their designs represented a fresh take on the highly ornamented style synonymous with bridal trousseaux and ethnic formal wear. One of these designers was Sabyasachi Mukherjee. His exponential success is centred around an opulent yet restrained interpretation of traditional bridal and ethnic formal wear.

Sabyasachi graduated from the National Institute of Fashion Technology (NIFT), Kolkata in 1999 and in 2001 won the Femina and British Council's Most Outstanding Young Designer of India award. He debuted at India Fashion Week in 2002. His first collections, such as 'Frog Princess' (2004) and 'The Nair Sisters' (Spring/Summer 2005), had a gypsy-bohemian aesthetic, which was very different from the ornate bridal and ethnic formal wear that began to define his collections from 2011 onwards.

Today, his bridal designs are highly coveted and considered to be a statement of social status and good taste. He evokes his Bengal heritage, forging an aesthetic steeped in Bengal's cultural history. His catwalk collections frequently explore the theme of the Raj and its influence on the dress of elite Bengal society.

According to Hindol Sengupta, in his cutting-edge exploration of the business of Indian fashion *Ramp Up* (2009), Sabyasachi was the first designer to break the Delhi stronghold on Indian design. Sengupta argues that in the 1990s the designer was for Delhi what the film star was for Mumbai. The North Indian Hindu Punjabi wedding was often a central feature in the popular romantic films of the great Bollywood directors such as Yash Chopra and thus had an enormous influence on the aesthetics of the bridal market. Much more recently, Sabyasachi has become the star designer for NDTV's reality makeover show *Band Baajaa Bride*, in which anxious brides-to-be from across India seek his magic touch to be made into the ideal Indian bride. A constant source of tension in these 'makeovers' is whether the bride wants to wear fashionable red *lehenga cholis* traditional to North Indian weddings or the traditional regional and ethnic clothes worn by their families. There is always a special sense of approval from Sabyasachi when a bride announces at the start of her makeover that she wants to wear something traditional and particular to her family traditions rather than red, although if she does insist on wearing a red *lehenga choli* he interprets this to pitch-perfect fashionable traditionalism. This reflects the tensions many brides face between wanting to be modern and on-trend and yet adhere to family expectations and local traditions.

right and below
'New Moon', PCJ
Delhi Couture Week,
2012.

Sabyasachi's store in south Mumbai's fort district is crammed with calendar images of gods and goddesses, artifacts and furniture assembled into an adept grammar of cultural heritage. The stores provide exquisitely beautiful spaces in which fantasy and culture can be experienced as a series of heightened sensory impressions curated to communicate the Sabyasachi brand and, at a deeper level, a sense of national pride mediated through traditional textiles and embroidery. His stores sell luxury in a gallery-like setting where fashion takes on a status akin to art, and heritage is commercialized in the concept of 'heirloom luxury'.

The biggest problem in India is that we have never believed in our strengths and we have looked upon the West for inspiration for the longest time. Luxury has a very specific mindset and you cannot create luxury from a point of subjugation. You have to create luxury from a leadership point of view. Therefore, if we as Indians do not look within ourselves and cannot find clothing solutions which exist within our own community, we will never be able to transcend and create an aspirational brand for all.

Sabyasachi is acutely aware of the challenges Indian designers face: many have often struggled to move past the 'couture' model of patronage and relatively small clientele to reach out across more lucrative market segments. When asked about his favourite designers he replies:

I appreciate the design team of Valentino: Maria Grazia Chiuri and Pierpaolo Piccioli. They make beautiful, sensible, wearable clothes, that are easy to comprehend by one and all, yet remain as aspiration to many. That is a tough balance to strike.

Sabyasachi has an antipathy towards bling and 'fashion'. Bling especially has connotations of an overwrought bridal- and Bollywood-driven market that many feel suffocates alternative

right
Lakmé Fashion
Week, Mumbai,
Summer 2011.

visions of Indian aesthetics in fashion. He champions hand-loom textiles and expertly executed traditional forms of embroidery. 'Sabyasachi wants to change the way India dresses' wrote Shefalee Vasudev, former editor of *Marie Claire India*, in her exposé of Indian fashion, *Powder Room* (2012).

Sabyasachi elevates craft to cultural heritage with a key role in defining India's place within domestic as well as potential international luxury markets. His fervent anti-fashion ethos is conveyed through frequent didactic pronouncements, which align him with the tradition of the famous couturier who dictates what should be worn. It is a didacticism underpinned by a politicized sense of fashion's role in constituting Indian identity, especially as Western brands continue to take hold in India. He believes that dressing should be an intellectual process and laments the crystal-embellished, skimpy outfits promoted by Bollywood. He has forged closed associations with actresses including Vidya Balan, a popular Hindi cinema actress known for taking on more challenging roles. He has often dressed her for red carpet events including Cannes, although in 2013 his styling of her with a head covering and *nath* (nose ring) ignited a furore, with one camp lauding her uber-traditional attire and the other claiming it represented a regressive image of Indian womanhood on the international stage.

If you look at Vidya, she is one of the few actresses who broke the mould by not looking and behaving in a certain way, endorsing beauty products, etc. When someone makes a statement like that – it is a strong, confident and rooted self that requires respect...the reason we did it was because it gave a very strong cultural identity to the clothing.

In India middle-class women in particular have had to bridge the wide gap between being at once a symbol of traditional domesticity and of independent modernity, spanning the gamut of roles from bride to wife, mother, homemaker and independent career woman. In the furore over Balan, much of which was played out on social media platforms such as Twitter and Facebook, what many read as a cultural nationalist conflation of Indian identity with an idealized image of womanhood was either lauded or derided. Popular blog *High Heel Confidential* summed it up succinctly:

Ah, Vidya (and her Sabyasachis) in Cannes! Fashion, feminism, playing to Western ideals of the 'exotic', bringing Indian craft to the forefront, too costume-y, making old-world poise and charm new-world sexy again... Whichever side of the debate you were on, a lot was said. Loathe it, love it, either way admit it.... It sure as hell was memorable!

Consistent in Mukherjee's creative practice is his design vision of Indian crafts forming

opposite
Actress Vidya Balan
on the cover of
Marie Claire,
October 2009. Stylist:
Shefalee Vasudev;
photograph:
Avinash Gowariker.

right
Lakmé Fashion
Week, Mumbai,
Autumn/Winter 2011.

a unique perspective on conspicuous consumption and luxury. He created an all-*khadi* bridal collection, taking the iconic textile at the heart of Gandhi's freedom movement against British rule, and reinventing it as modern-day luxury.[11] Mukherjee has often stated he wants to 'teach good taste to the rich' and his work continues the legacy of both pre- and post-colonial support of Indian decorative arts and crafts as a form of nation making, intimately bound up in the class position and taste practices of the English-speaking elite milieu who lived in Calcutta (now Kolkata), Bengal.[12] His collections are given evocative titles that underscore this highly political sense of Indian luxury as grounded in the unique cultural heritage of his native Bengal, including *Aparajito (Bengali: the Unvanquished)* in 2010; the 'Unvanquished' being a reference to India's heritage of textiles and his vision to sustain them in the frame of contemporary fashion.

Traditional crafts are very important to me, such as khadi. *They are the soul and DNA of my brand. My brand supports many weaving communities in India which were dying out and although I don't want to sound like somebody on a social mission, it gives me the greatest joy and fulfilment when my company contributes to the revival of craft.*

In 2010 Sabyasachi started a reasonably priced line of hand-loom saris packaged in cylindrical tins decorated with sepia images of 19th-century Bengal. Branded as his 'Save the Sari' product line, he develops textiles with weavers' co-operative societies across India.

Four years ago I went on a trip to Pochampally to source cotton and silk saris. It is there that I realized that a family of four makes less than Rs 4,000 a month (approx 50 euros). Half the money is eaten by middlemen and also the pressures of the fashion industry have a big impact on it as well. That's when I decided to pick up the cost as part of a CSR initiative of curating and reviving Indian saris and selling them at

a zero overhead business model, only adding freight, local taxes and packaging.

He envisions creating an 'intellectually aspirational global super brand'. In 2012, Sabyasachi, along with Rohit Bal, attracted investment from L Capital, the private equity investment arm of French luxury conglomerate Louis Vuitton Moët Hennessy (LVMH).

Sabyasachi has secured his place as a highly talented designer whose keen business sense is grounded in an acute political sense of India's role as a key non-Western fashion destination.

opposite
Campaign image for the 'Ferozabad' collection shown at Shree Raj Mahal Jewellers India Couture Week, 2014. Shiny metallic elements were incorporated into Sabyasachi's signature aesthetic, evoking a nostalgic, sepia-hued image of aristocratic Indian history.

top left, right and bottom left
Models backstage wearing designs for 'Ferozabad', Shree Raj Mahal Jewellers India Couture Week, 2014. Photograph: Nitin Patel for thebigfatindian wedding.com.

bottom right
Campaign image for 'Ferozabad', 2014.

Anamika Khanna

opposite
PCJ Delhi Couture
Week, 2013.

below
Signature cape and
reinvention of
traditional draped
dhoti into on-trend
pants, PCJ Delhi
Couture Week, 2013.

In 2012, fashion house Chanel showed
a collection on the Paris catwalk called
'Paris-Bombay'. Models wore *maang tikkas*
on their foreheads and Indian-inspired
silhouettes rendered with the severe but
opulent signature style of Chanel. It was
a dynamic dialogue between Western
luxury and globally circulating images
of India. Creative director Karl Lagerfeld

commented, 'If there isn't a modern touch,
then it's just a costume show.' He also
observed that Indian women – the kind
who can buy Chanel – 'always mix it with
something from India, they don't have to
renounce their own style because they
have a strong one, they can add something,
but they always stay Indian.'

One key aspect of this push and pull
of influences, and fashion's dynamic
role in actively negotiating an authentic
Indian identity through clothing, is in
the assertion of what constitutes 'good'
taste. Often taste is created along the
lines of negative differentiation from
another group, and in the context of Indian
luxury fashion it is also part of a complex
dynamic with the West. Anamika Khanna
has carved a unique space in the market
for luxury bridal and ethnic formal wear.
Her designs are often called 'restrained',
highlighting the place of her work as
part of a conversation with the broader
market context of *filmi*, blingy Bollywood-
influenced fashion. Of Khanna's designs
writer Shefalee Vasudev says, 'They are
strongly Indian in a non-ethnic way',
while Sujata Assomull Sippy at V*ogue
India* wrote of Khanna's 2012 Couture
Week collection, 'These were certainly not
static, heavy, portrait-style clothing pieces.
Lightness was important.'

It is the dialogue Khanna creates
between fluid, pared-back traditional
Indian garments, luxurious fabrication and
Western silhouettes that demonstrates her
ability to move fluently between local and
global idioms of fashion. Of the tendency
to create labels based on the idea of fusion
she is emphatic:

*I somehow do not understand the word
'Indo-Western'. It actually irritates me, as
does 'ethno-chic'. Well, what we have is simply
modern, stylish, subtle clothing, sometimes
inspired by only India, sometimes the world....
If I am true to my design, surely, who I am,
where I come from, the people around me,
my background – all of it is bound to influence*

'With Love From Taj', part of a project commissioned by the Taj Mahotsav Committee (Uttar Pradesh Tourism). Photograph: taken at the Taj Mahal, Agra by Pravin Talan.

above
The cape is part of Khanna's signature approach to occasion dressing. Stylist: Nidhi Jacob; photograph: Arjun Mark for *Elle India*, November 2013.

The sari has always been an object of fascination for me. Nowhere in the world can an unstitched yard of fabric be worn in so many styles. However, to let its essence refrain from becoming a costume, I felt it important to make it easier to wear, smart and stylish, without disrespecting what it stands for. Thus, the half-drape sari.

The relationship between traditional Indian silhouettes and contemporary Western ideas of combining separates informs Khanna's approach to design. She draws on traditional shapes, for instance, the *dhoti* shape is an inspiration for her luxury high-waisted draped trousers. She treats *bandhgalas* and *sherwanis* like modern jackets, or reinvents the classic Rajasthani gathered top in terms of Western fashion concepts such as the peplum top. Khanna believes in interpreting traditional Indian silhouettes in a modern way. In the waistcoat, especially, she finds a 'versatile and smart shape...to play around with, dressing up or down with this one piece is easy.'

Khanna is deeply reflective about what exactly defines couture in India today, considering its synonymous associations with bridal wear in the Indian luxury market, yet seeking to redefine it in terms of her own design vision.

I draw inspiration from Indian history, crafts and textiles, respecting the uniqueness and the vast empire of culture that I have; however, looking at it in a contemporary, modern and more evolved form. Not shying away from the fact that

my work. I come from Rajasthan, and now live in modern surroundings. My family, while modern in lifestyle, also has a deep-rooted respect for our culture and traditions. I would think my work surely is influenced by all of it.

One of her key signature pieces is the half-drape sari which combines ease of movement and a fluid, linear silhouette, instantly recognizable as a Khanna design.

We always start a story with a traditional Indian shape. Looking at the Indian lehenga like a skirt, teaming it with a jacket, or layering a cape over a sari.

subtle elements of gold- or silver-wire embroidery. For each new collection her creative process involves a distillation of her inspirations, which, she says, can be anything from

...the wings of butterflies, a collection of historical costumes, old textiles, old monuments ...anything...every collection involves a large amount of research and development, whether historical European costumes or African tribes. The marriage of those outside to what I have here in India is what gets the adrenalin going.

below left
Freida Pinto at
A Small World
Foundation winter
weekend, Gstaad,
Switzerland, 2013.
Photograph: Billy
Farrell of BFANYC.

below right
Embroidered top
and jacket with
divided *dhoti* pants,
PCJ Delhi Couture
Week, 2012.

our world extends beyond the boundaries of this country. Clearly our signature would imply subtlety, the use of Indian craft in extremely modern, experimental, versatile styles.

Ornamentation is also a key part of Khanna's design signature but it is often rendered sparingly and in monochromatic pairings across her designs. She also favours *aari* work and Lucknowi *mukaish* which combines the traditional white-on-white *chikankari* threadwork with

Khanna started with the idea of an Indian brand selling internationally, which was a completely new concept.

In India we have our own rules and somehow here 'more is less'. Classic example, the first time when I was in London with my collection, a lady wanted to buy a coat to hang it on the wall; that's when I realized it's about editing, clarity of thought and courage after all.

Crafting and weaving Indian fashion

opposite
Hand-woven wild
silk jacket, Abraham
& Thakore, Autumn/
Winter 2014.

below
NGOs such as
WomenWeave in
Madhya Pradesh run
by Sally Holkar aim to
make traditional hand-
loom and craft relevant
for contemporary fashion
markets. Sustainable
livelihoods and fair
pay for rural craft
workers are at the
heart of such initiatives.

Craft in all its rich diversity is integral to the work of many Indian designers. Whether in the embroideries adorning regal bridal wear, as illustrated in the previous chapter, or in simple hand-spun and woven cottons, tactile weaves of wild silk or the intricate patterns of hand-loom *ikat* saris. This chapter explores design innovation in hand-woven textiles. At a global level, ethical and sustainable fashion has drawn small-scale craft-based forms of production into the spotlight as community-based solutions to issues of fair labour and environmental resource depletion. India has a unique history of craft-based design intervention, ripe for translation into these global concerns through the material practices of high fashion.

right
Sally Holkar, the founder
of WomenWeave,
has also set up the
pioneering Handloom
School in Maheshwar,
Madhya Pradesh. The
school aims to educate
weavers in design,
textile technology,
fashion and language
to equip them for
working in contemporary
fashion markets.

Historically, hand-spun and hand-woven cloth, known as *khadi*, and the ideal of Swadeshi (where production is based in one's own country) formed the backbone for Mahatma Gandhi's anti-colonial movement seeking an independent, economically self-sufficient nation. In the post-independence era, *khadi* and hand-loom products have been the focus of a raft of government initiatives run by a labyrinthine state bureaucracy attempting to connect the livelihoods of rural weavers with urban consumer markets in the name of rural development and the ideological goal of nation building. Yet often craft has languished in dusty government-run emporiums or has been aimed at the tourist market in

below
Detail of a Rahul Mishra
dress from 'The Similar
Opposites', Wills Lifestyle
India Fashion Week,
Autumn/Winter 2012.
As well as hand-
woven textiles, many
designers also work with
traditional embroidery
techniques, using them
as part of addressing
the technical challenges
of fabrication with
hand-loom and
infusing embroidery
with contemporary
design aesthetics.

the form of cheap mass-produced craft products, attracting criticism that many initiatives serve only to devalue craft, undermining the skilled labour necessary for sustaining the continuity of craft traditions.

Since the 1980s, there has been a shift in approaches to craft, reflecting both the government's attempts to develop high value added global markets for craft, the work of key advocates of craft such as Martand Singh, Rahul Jain, Rta Kapur Chishti and Jaya Jaitly as well as institutional design education. All of the designers in this chapter studied at either The National Institute of Design (NID) in Ahmedabad, renowned for its founding philosophy that envisages design as a tool for solving social problems and enabling rural livelihoods, or at National Institute of Fashion Technology (NIFT), which has fifteen campuses across India. NIFT is considered to be a more 'fashion'-orientated educational institution, but it is nonetheless run under the auspices of the Indian Ministry of Textiles and craft documentation forms an integral part of its curriculum.

Craft is integral to the evolving identity of Indian fashion and there now exists a corpus of Indian designers who hold an uncontested place as innovators in translating indigenous and traditional hand-loom into seasonal collections. Yet their individual approaches remain highly distinctive. In this chapter we focus on the designers who are renowned for their work with weavers of traditional hand-loom cloth. In their innovative work with weavers, their design ideation and the ways that they brand and market their craft-based fashion, wider issues of modernity and tradition are always in a dynamic dialogue through material practices of craft and fashion. Some designers take the purist approach of using traditional Indian dress forms, such as the tunic-like *kurta* or loose *salwar* trousers, and reinventing them in terms of global fashion concepts, such as anti-fit clothing, or transforming them with more tailored construction and detailing. They do so in conjunction with stripping traditional hand-loom weaves back to minimal or graphic woven patterns and work with the same craftspeople across seasons to produce highly refined hand-loom textiles.

opposite
'Shaadi Redux' at Wills Lifestyle India
Fashion Week, Autumn/Winter 2013.

Abraham & Thakore

Since the 1980s, Abraham & Thakore (A&T) has produced textile-based fashion that makes them both 'designer's designers' in the arena of fashion and highly respected among the experts and practitioners in the rarefied arena of Indian craft advocacy. Abraham & Thakore is made up of creative director David Abraham, a Singapore-born designer, director Rakesh Thakore, who was born in Delhi and spent his early childhood in East Africa, and Kevin Nigli, who manages A&T's participation at international trade and Indian fashion shows. They have three stand-alone stores in Bangalore, Mumbai and Delhi.

'Abraham & Thakore' is a byword for well-cut, minimal clothing made from hand-loom textiles. Their pioneering approach to design involves questioning what constitutes fashion and a production model based on the lead times necessary to work with hand-woven textiles. Their goal is to interpret traditional hand-loom textiles, with their distinctive regional and cultural identities, in new ways for the contemporary urban consumer. This, however, is not straightforward in a retail market where crystals and bling on a sari often commands a higher price than a painstakingly hand-woven one.

Abraham & Thakore's Autumn/Winter 2011 collection was based on the influence of menswear on women's fashion.

right
Hand-woven *ikat kurta*, Autumn/ Winter 2011. Inspired by traditional menswear, Abraham & Thakore reinvented traditional *ikat* weaving to replicate the pattern of houndstooth tweed.

far right
Hand-woven *ikat* 'houndstooth' sari worn with a chartreuse skirt, Autumn/Winter 2011.

above, left to right
Minimal, fluid and understated separates in high-quality hand-loom textiles define the brand.

opposite
'Urban Shikar', Wills Lifestyle India Fashion Week, Delhi, Autumn/Winter 2014.

Houndstooth itself has an established tradition of reinvention in fashion design history, from Dior's oversized tweed in the 1950s to Alexander McQueen's subversion of houndstooth with 'Horn of Plenty', Autumn/Winter 2009. Abraham & Thakore's graphic houndstooth sari with an acid chartreuse border commented on the sari's role in the contemporary working woman's wardrobe and, again, subtly reinstated the relationship between Indian craft and Western idioms of fashion, which stretch back to the era of colonial British rule and the adoption by Indian elites of Western dress: the Western man's suit, in particular, when tweeds such as houndstooth became part of the repertoire of men's clothing.

The wildcard in this collection was what appeared to be a tessellated houndstooth print, but was in fact finely woven by craftsmen known for creating the *ikat* saris of Andhra Pradesh and Orissa. The *ikat* weaving process is an exercise in complex dye-resist methods that demand highly skilled expertise, passed down through the generations. It is only when woven on the loom that the pattern concealed in the resist-dyed yarn unfolds into the distinctive

ikat patterns. Yet with the declining number of women who wear saris across India, the future of such sari-weaving traditions is uncertain. It is important to find ways to translate these traditional techniques across to contemporary markets – this is the focus of a number of NGO, government and design industry movements in India today.

Abraham & Thakore have never done bridal wear, their pared-back aesthetic and unadorned surfaces are generally unsuited to it. However, for Wills Lifestyle India Fashion Week, Autumn/Winter 2013 they collaborated with Ekaya, one of the most established textile manufacturers of Benaras brocades in Varanasi, and produced 'Shaadi Redux', a collection based on Benaras brocade silk. Associated with bridal wear, the brocades are decorated with paisley, floral, bird and animal motifs.

We were interested in experimenting with the design vocabulary and using the technique to create simple geometric patterns based on graphic interpretations of the interweaving of the warp and weft threads but simultaneously retaining the complex weaving techniques.

'The streets of a city are the terrain, a smartphone the defence. Shaped by a palette based on the golden hues of wild silk, the collection evokes the many shades of khaki with its references to safari, uniforms and combat', from concept note for 'Urban Shikar', Wills Lifestyle India Fashion Week, 2014.

above
Autumn/Winter 2014.

above right
'Urban Shikar',
Autumn/Winter 2014.

right
Wills Lifestyle India
Fashion Week,
Autumn/Winter 2014.

This traditional textile was given
a characteristically modern twist,
transforming the elaborate patterns into
graphic checks and Abraham & Thakore's
favoured monochromatic signature palette
of black against neutrals, an extra boost
of luxe injected with metallic golds. Their
goal was to make it 'rich', but not 'blingy':
a crucial aesthetic statement for these
renowned hand-loom-orientated designers
in a wider market context where Bollywood
and, more latterly, the hugely popular
genre of TV soap operas have driven a
mass retail fashion and bridal market
dominated by chiffon, crystals

right
Autumn/Winter 2014.

below left and right
Wills Lifestyle India
Fashion Week,
Autumn/Winter 2014.

and synthetic fabrics encrusted with gold-coloured embroidery.

For Wills India Fashion Week, Autumn/Winter 2014, Abraham & Thakore again focused on *ikat* and took wild silk yarn to different weavers, including *jamdani* weavers of Fulia in Bengal, who wove the silk using a traditional three-shuttle technique to create modern geometrics based on the classic temple motif of woven Indian textiles abstracted into graphic shapes and patterns. For the first time ever they also included leopard print, a perennial trend on international catwalks, but given a unique twist by embroidering or digitally printing it on tactile wild silk, hand-woven saris. Again, traditional crafts and silhouettes were skilfully combined with fashionable trends, yet these are trends appropriated on Abraham & Thakore's terms into a profound design process of directional hand-loom-based fashion.

Wendell Rodricks

opposite
Model Ujjwala Raut
wears a blouse
from 'Isadora India'
Spring/Summer
2006. Photograph:
Farrokh Chothia.

right
Model Yashmin in
a jacket from 'Les
Vamp', Spring/
Summer 2007.
Photograph:
Vishesh Verma.

Wendell Rodricks is a veteran designer who was instrumental in creating institutions such as Lakmé Fashion Week which helped a consolidated Indian fashion industry emerge. In 2013 Rodricks was awarded the Padma Shri, India's highest civilian honour, for his contribution to Indian fashion and textile traditions. He has written an autobiography, *The Green Room* (2012), and *Moda Goa* (2012), an in-depth history of Goan costume and textiles. In the latter Rodricks explores the multi-faceted history of Goa through its local dress styles. He discusses, for example, how 16th-century Portuguese conquerors adapted their traditional Renaissance dress to cope with the hot Konkan climate and the ways in which newly converted Goan Catholics adopted Western dress.

Rodricks' design approach provides a different view of Goa, looking beyond the tourist hotspots popularized from the 1960s onwards and into the heart of Goa's rich landscape, culture, ethnic and religious history. He was brought up in Mumbai and studied design in America and France, but he returned to the Goan ancestral village of his family in the 1990s.

Here, with a life steeped in local cuisine, literature and architecture, Rodricks forged a signature style, based on fluid drapes, minimal detailing and the colour white, which often dominates his collections. Fluidity and effortless glamour are his defining design tropes, inspired by the ecology and cultural pulse of Goa as well as his cutting technique based on ancient Indian geometry and indigenous methods of draping unstitched cloth on the bias.

His hand-loom textiles translated into fluid drapes and sinuous cuts represent his conversation with both Indian design and Western fashion. In the 1980s Rodricks first created a style that was born of a rejection of what he calls the 'Maharaja look' (predominantly evident in highly ornamented bridal wear) as well as the influence of the formal Western men's dress in India from the 18th century onwards. He fused traditional ethnic wear with a relaxed, cosmopolitan sensibility: sharp-shouldered yet light, loose-fitting men's jackets were among his signature pieces.

Rodricks' work has included reviving the weaving of *kunbi* saris, which languished when the Portuguese, who ruled Goa

opposite
Actress Lakshmi
Menon in a gown
from 'Les Vamp'
Spring/Summer
2007. Photograph:
Prabuddha
Dasgupta.

right
Freida Pinto on
the catwalk at
'Les Vamp',
Lakmé Fashion
Week, Mumbai,
Spring/Summer
2007.

below right
'Water Spray'
collection,
Lakmé Fashion
Week, Mumbai,
finale, 2003.
Photograph:
Vishesh Verma.

overleaf
Evelyn Sharma
with Wendell
Rodricks. She
is wearing one
of his signature
fluid creations.
Photograph: Arjun
Mark for *Hello!*
magazine.

for over two hundred years, banned the
wearing of them. As the British had banned
weaving across India to encourage imports
of Manchester cloth, so the Portuguese
wanted Goans to buy cloth from which
they would profit. Rodricks' historical
research surely informs his design practice
– he sees the continuity of the implications
of foreign trade when he reflects on
contemporary India.

*We have a large local market to satisfy.
The world is aware that in a few years we
will have the largest young consumer market.
Foreign labels want to tap into this market,
so we need to organize ourselves to satisfy
the local market or we will be overrun by
cheap international brands.*

The world is aware that in a few years we will have the largest young consumer market…we need to organize ourselves to satisfy the local market or we will be overrun by cheap international brands.

opposite
'Source of Youth'
collection at Wills
Lifestyle India
Fashion Week, 2014.

right
Jesse Randhawa in
a bias-cut gown for
the 'Ocean Oriente'
collection, the finale
of the Wendell
Rodricks show,
Wills Lifestyle India
Fashion Week,
Delhi, 2013.

opposite
Man's World magazine.
Photograph: Bikramjit Bose.

below
Bollywood actor Milind Soman
in a white cotton shirt –
a Pratap Singh signature.

Rajesh Pratap Singh

Rajesh Pratap Singh has a reputation
for having a sophisticated, pared-down
aesthetic, without the use of ornamentation
to augment the luxurious hand-loom
weaves he invests with dedicated attention
to technical development.

*The purity in the traditional textile is what one
needs to work with for a modern interpretation,
and that is what I try to do all the time, the
reason being, I love doing this.*

He worked with David Abraham while
he was still studying at NIFT and after
graduating in 1994 he worked in a
menswear company producing tailoring
for an Italian brand. In 1997, he started his
own label in Delhi.

*There were no fashion weeks at that time but
the industry was gaining a structure by some
of the senior designers present then.*

Pratap Singh does not design bridal wear,
which makes his continued commercial
success and the high esteem in which he
is held by the design fraternity all the
more notable. He is renowned for his work
with textiles.

*Hand-loom is a key element in what we do;
it is important because yarn makes the basic*

*structure of what we try to create. It is more
important than any other ornamentation, the
process of making yarn is mesmerizing and we
will continue to learn about it.*

He is deeply immersed in the R&D process
and for the last 16 years has worked to
develop traditional textiles such as *khadi*,
employing his own weavers on-site at his
factory and producing a fine 600-thread
count *khadi* made from handturned
and hand-woven yarn. He does not
feel, however, that his output needs to
be governed by the Gandhian ideal of
Swadeshi, which promoted hand-spun,
hand-woven cotton as the fabric of self-
sufficiency and as a political statement
against foreign imports.

*It would be a very boring world if everything
looked the same! Swadeshi is important, it's
in many ways what we are trying to do, but we
don't want to restrict ourselves to say that we
will never use polyester, or machine-made yarn.
I find that view really dated, we need to blend
the two, we need to see what works, and in a
sensible way.... It's about something being pure,
it can be from anywhere.*

this page
'Ikat' collection,
Spring/Summer 2014.

We are working with lots of textiles: linen, wool, cotton yarns, stainless steel, paper, silver, we are experimenting all the time.... Much of our work is with hand-loom but certain techniques use some basic machine-made yarns.

Pratap Singh's openness to the relationship between hand-loom and technical innovation in synthetic fabrics is part of his broader approach to sustainable design.

A serious amount of research needs to go into it, polyester can be more sustainable than cotton! There are so may factors such as dyes, fertilisers, length of consumer-use...maybe we need to go really high-tech in certain areas to make it sustainable, all the BT cotton grown in India is anything but sustainable because it's killing our soil! Sustainability is not just important, it's that we don't have a choice!

Juxtaposing severe tailoring with fluid draping is one of his design signatures in addition to the skilled execution of cut and construction in his work. He also takes traditional craft techniques such as *ajrak* printing and gives them surprising new twists. Intricate *ajrak* motifs printed in earthy hues across his 2010 Van Heusen menswear collection in Delhi turned out on closer inspection to contain small skull motifs. Traditionally, the skull has associations with death, fearsome Hindu goddesses and tantric rituals in India, but its international image has been influenced by its adoption as part of the sub-culture of rock music and the absorption of this motif into the often dark creative universe of British designer Alexander McQueen. Divia Patel records the process by which Pratap Singh realized the skull motifs, finding that traditional *ajrak* artisans refused to carve skull motifs due to their taboo in Muslim religion, instead they were digitally printed.[13]

For the catwalk show at Van Heusen Men's Fashion Week 2010 Pratap Singh used 'real' models: musicians from India's

this page
'Ikat' collection, Spring/Summer 2014. Black-and-white patterns of polka dots, rings, diamonds and colour blocking have been created using traditional hand-woven *ikat* techniques with lightweight silks and cotton.

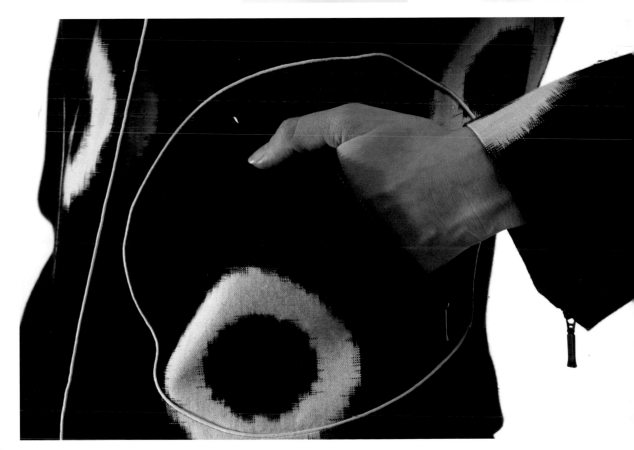

*We are not Gandhi, we can never be
Gandhi, so we will stick to our business
and what we can do...*

**opposite above
left and right
and below right**
Van Heusen Men's
Fashion Week,
Delhi, 2010.

opposite below left
Woman's jacket
showing the digital
ajrak print of
entwined flowers
and human skulls,
2010.

counter culture of rock bands. The
audience clapped and cheered as
the musicians swaggered insouciantly
down a catwalk covered with calf hide.

*There was again a twist to the traditional craft,
for me it was the late 1960s and 1970s classic
rock 'n' roll imagery which we tried to play
around with by referencing how craft became
part of the style at that point in time. It was in
the 1960s when block prints seeped into the
scene – that was what we were trying to project
and, yes, we still do like rock 'n' roll!*

Evident here is the referencing of India
as it was refracted through Western
eyes and, again, there is a sense of
irony, play and reclaiming these motifs
in terms of a contemporary, cosmopolitan
Indian identity. Pratap Singh's designs
often have an edginess that seems to
challenge the observer to ask, whose
symbols are these, what is 'Indian'
or 'Western' – is this a Western view
of India, or a playful post-modern
pastiche of a Western view with
a new twist, a personal biography,
a wider social commentary on what
it means to be Indian in an ever more
globalized world?
　　Pastiche, irony and iconicity are all
concepts that an ethnographer, fashion
theorist or journalist can read from Pratap
Singh's work, but concepts from which

this famously reticent designer would shy
away. In magazine interviews his answers
may come across as a little taciturn, or
even brusque, but in person there is a shy,
reserved gentleness about him. Perhaps
he is economical with words because he
is a purist through and through, not only
in his design approach but also in his
refusal to flatter the need for spin and
chatter that propels the fashion media.
The fashion media often describes him as
'Indo-gothic' or as embodying 'minimalist
Western tailoring'.

*The press love to put people in categories and
so do the marketing teams worldwide. I am
a designer based in India who designs products
which can be used both in India and outside.
We want to make new things every season
and because of our visual references that have
been derived from India, our product has those
echoes, but it has nothing to do with clichéd
Indian imagery.*

A great admirer of the work of Abraham
& Thakore, his own work is influenced by

*Purity and an attempt for contribution. One of
the satisfactions coming out of fashion is you
have many hundreds of people and their families
dependent on you and that is a huge motivation
each day. We are not Gandhi, we can never be
Gandhi, so we will stick to our business and
what we can do...*

Samant Chauhan

In the work of Bihar-born and Delhi-based Samant Chauhan, we find an intense and often rebellious dialogue with prevailing aesthetic codes of Indian fashion. His collections are distinctive for their monochromatic ivory palette made from Bhagalpur tussah (raw silk) woven

by weavers from Chauhan's native state. A graduate of NIFT, Delhi, in 2007 his first collection 'Kamasutra' attracted plaudits from important figures including FDCI president Sunil Sethi, who said it was 'ingenious', and Didier Grumbach, then Chairman of the Chambre Syndicale de la Haute Couture, who declared Chauhan 'one to watch'.

Chauhan is from Bihar, a beleaguered Indian State with headline-grabbing levels of poverty, political corruption and criminality. He is keen to act as an ambassador for his native state, portraying a different image of Bihar which is grounded in its craft traditions, sites of Buddhist pilgrimage and outstanding architectural heritage. He champions Bhagalpur silk and his creative process centres on this distinctive raw silk, which is left un-dyed, so his collections are monochromatic, very different from the bright hues that usually dominate Indian fashion. When Chauhan first came to study at NIFT in affluent South Delhi it was a 'culture shock'. He recalls feeling judged by his peers, who stereotyped him as a backward country boy:

They couldn't believe I was someone from Bihar who wore Levi jeans. They asked how someone from Bihar could possibly know about such fashionable things.

Chauhan's background fits with broader themes of social mobility in contemporary India and fashion's power to afford personal transformation, even grant dreams and riches. He is one of the newer generation of designers who benefited from the 'democratization' of design through educational institutions such as NIFT, where previously personal wealth and family connections were often the only route for aspiring designers.[14]

His early collections were experiments in edgy streetwear, often using shock tactics that turned the catwalk into moments of theatre, garnering media attention.

above and opposite
From the lookbook
for 'The Silk Route',
Wills Lifestyle India
Fashion Week,
Autumn/Winter
2009. Photographs:
Raghubir Singh.

'Kamasutra', Chauhan's first collection after graduating, featured digital images of erotic Khajuraho Temple sculptures from Madhya Pradesh. Chauhan's use of Khajuraho imagery translates civilizational heritage into commodified visual culture. As anthropologist Christopher Pinney writes, this use of historic imagery 'should not be interpreted as some organic wellspring of a Hindu symbolic unconscious', but instead as 'consciously creative ensembles that strive for deliberately allegorical effect'.[15] In this vein, Chauhan's 'Kamasutra' collection is an example of what anthropologist William Mazzarella terms auto-orientalism and the Kamasutra's long history of orientalist appropriation means its use as part of fashion imagery translates to international as well as domestic audiences.[16] Using this imagery was part of Chauhan's strategy to raise the profile of Bhagalpur silk as a luxury textile with high fashion potential.

Courses on sustainable fashion are a recent development in the UK, but they have a longer history in India, where specific meanings and practices of sustainable fashion are systematized within institutions such as NIFT and The National Institute of Design (NID). Chauhan reflects that he first came to know of Bhagalpur silk from his native state through craft documentation modules integral to the NIFT curriculum. Fashion college not only shaped him into an urbane young man, but also gave him the tools to reinvent his regional identity in terms of the ethnic branding of Bhagalpur silk.

The coarse hand-woven silk from Bihar became a point of allegorical departure for this young designer. His ethnic rootedness was transformed into the potential of its seductive representation and moral claims to powerful ideas of craft, national pride and a uniquely Indian form of luxury silk in urban markets.

Like many of the designers whose work blurs the boundaries between fashion design and craft advocacy, a distinct interpretation of sustainable livelihoods form a core part of his design vision. In 2009 he participated in 'The Shared Talent India Project' at the Centre for Sustainable Fashion (part of the London College of Fashion) sharing learning on ethical and sustainable practices. Chauhan speaks of the idiosyncrasies of raw silk in terms of improving weaver's livelihoods.

The challenge with Bhagalpur silk is to allow the silkworm to cut the cocoon and come out, but the yarn filament gets eaten through, cut, so that means it takes hundreds of cocoons to make a metre of silk, and the shorter strands of filament make the hand spinning process very difficult. The thickness of the yarn is very uneven and that in turn causes problems during the weaving, so it takes a very balanced, very experienced craftsman to do this. But in the last ten years Bhagalpur weavers have started importing yarn from China and using that as warp. They can make this fabric faster, cheaper, with more profit, but the look and feel of the silk is totally different. But the weavers don't understand the long-term implications, that they can't compete with the Chinese silk market. So this is the problem.

But his unbending vision of raw monochromatic silk has often been

The challenge with Bhagalpur silk is to allow the silkworm to cut the cocoon and come out, but the yarn filament gets eaten through, cut, so that means it takes hundreds of cocoons to make a metre of silk.

Here a wrap jacket is made from tussah silk interwoven with fine stripes of zari (gold thread) and decorated with french knot embroidery.

above left
Detail from zari
embroidered cotton
bodice. Courtesy
of Pernia's pop-up
shop.

above centre
Organza silk-and-
organdy pleated
gown with silk
thread and gold zari
floral embroidered
net bodice and
sheer detailing.
'Rajputana Dream',
Wills Lifestyle India
Fashion Week,
Spring/Summer 2015.

above right
'Rajputana Dream',
Wills Lifestyle India
Fashion Week,
Spring/Summer 2015.

challenging. It represents a unique stance in the aesthetics and commercial realities of the Indian fashion industry.

In India the client is still very much occasion oriented, they are going to spend money like hell for a wedding or party…. If I start doing the same thing for the weddings I start making money, but I start losing my brand identity. It's very tricky. Maybe later on I can work out a way to do it.

Indeed by 2011, Chauhan had launched his first bridal wear line, while almost completely retaining his distinctive monochromatic palette and introducing fresh interpretations of traditional *zardosi* embroidery. His 2013 collection 'Rajputana Biker' saw a technical development with different blends of raw silk, embroidered with bird-wing motifs inspired by the tattoos of bikers who ride vintage Enfields across Rajasthan. His signature take on women's ethnic silhouettes includes flared

anarkalis, dipped asymmetrical hemlines lined in rich red silk, which add drama to his all-ivory palette, and full-skirted gowns with bodices structured and fitted close to the body using embroidery. In successive Rajputana bridal line collections he has continued to experiment with the balance between lustrous expanses of raw silk and ornamentation, and a particular way he does this is though decorative embroidery placements that take trailing vines, flowers and birds as inspiration. In this way, he forges a distinctive voice within Indian fashion, melding the philosophy of hand-loom with an innovative interpretation of the aesthetic norms of Indian bridal wear. With the opening of two flagship stores in Delhi and Bihar, it would seem Chauhan has been able to achieve his goal of expanding commercially while staying true to his design vision based on the luxurious potential of raw Bhagalpur silk.

opposite
Actress Shruti wears an ivory
organza hand-embroidered
jacket, Spring/Summer 2014.
Photograph: R. Burman for
Harper's Bazaar Bride India.

Rahul Mishra

below
Reversible dress
showcases hand-
loom Kerala cloth
woven by Hindus
in south India; the
other side reveals
rich Banarasi silk
woven by Muslims
in the north.
Photograph:
Abhijit Bhatle.

Rahul Mishra is a passionate individual:
some might say he is passionate to the
point of obsession. His college peers say
he was always like this, even as a young
student at NID in Ahmedabad. Talking
to Mishra about his design practice is
like talking to an engineer about the
complexities of technical specifications
and the challenges of research and design
– melding the exactitude of a scientist with
an artist's vision, he is a skilled technician
of both silhouette and textile development.

He grew up in Uttar Pradesh in a middle-
class family and recalls that when he
attended school in the late 1980s it cost
seven rupees a month and when it rained
water would seep through the wall of the
mud-rendered building. After graduating
in physics from Kanpur University, he
attended NID and followed its founding
mission of design for social and
sustainable development. In his words,
'Everything that guides my design vision
I owe to studying there'. He graduated in
2005 and was awarded NID's Best Student
Designer of the Year award. He went on
to win a highly competitive scholarship
to study for an MA in Fashion at the
Milan-based Istituto Marangoni (he was
the first non-European designer to be
awarded one of these scholarships). Here,
he honed his design skills and overcame
his sense of being intimidated by famous
brands, becoming familiar with the global
vocabulary of high fashion. In 2008, he
returned to India. He insists that first and
foremost, he's a designer searching for
solutions for hand-loom textiles. Each
season he reinvents signature textiles,
design motifs and silhouettes.

His scientific approach to the
technical development of hand-loom and
fabrication reflects his intense intellectual
engagement with the design process. Each
of his collections involves story-telling
and his collection titles use witty acronyms
to express his vision of the relationship
between fashion, craft, livelihoods and
the environment. Mishra transforms hand-
loom textiles into silhouettes that represent
a sophisticated dialogue between
traditional ethnic and Western wear.

*To understand hand-loom one must understand
the structure: the weave is irregular, making
embroideries upon its surface more difficult.
The challenge is to bring the two things
together...hand-loom, it comes with a strong
identity as a designer, crafts lead the way. Any
craft has taken millions of minds to bring it to its
present state. A textile speaks to me, guides me.*

His particular ability to use complex
fabrication to translate hand-loom fabrics,

The moment I see his creation on the ramp... you're familiar with the fabric, but you're not familiar with the whole silhouette.... There is a simplicity...and yet anybody who understands textiles will see the complexity whether it is in the weave or in the construction or the detailing.

Mishra's 2010 collection 'The Butterfly Effect' was inspired by mathematician Edward Lorenz's chaos theory, which hypothesizes that small but significant changes can have exponential effects, an idea popular in explaining the causes and impacts of climate change. He combined these ideas with inspiration from graphic artist M. C. Escher's metamorphosis prints and created densely embroidered pieces in which lifeforms mutated and transformed from organic forms into urban landscapes and back again. This symbolized the designer's ambitious vision of the role of Indian craft in forging a sustainable and ethical solution to issues of poverty and environmental resource depletion.

For his prize-winning 2014 International Woolmark Prize entry, Mishra turned his attention to merino wool and revisited the idea of chaos theory and metamorphosis. He honed it into a more aesthetically developed and refined theme by creating urban landscapes in metamorphosis, using wool yarn to embroider densely intricate shapes emulating the petals of the lotus, India's national flower and a spiritual symbol of purity and enlightenment.

Before a panel of judges Mishra made the presentation of wool transformed into unexpectedly delicate embroidered cocktail dresses and spoke with characteristic emotion of his desire to create sustainable livelihoods for the weavers and craftworkers with whom he collaborates. His ethos echoes that most Gandhian of statements, 'Recall the face of the poorest and the weakest man whom you may have seen and ask yourself if the step you contemplate is going to be of any use to him.'

above
'The Similar Opposites', Wills Lifestyle India Fashion Week, Autumn/Winter 2012.

such as fine and semi-transparent *chanderi*, into tailored fusion silhouettes was evident early on in his career. He has a sophisticated way of employing layered and fine woven *chanderi*, cut on the bias and structured into fitted jackets and bodices, from which flow semi-transparent skirts to make a virtue out of the often challenging proclivities of fine hand-loom weaves. After Mishra's Autumn/Winter 2011 show at Wills Lifestyle India Fashion Week, Sunil Sethi, President of the FDCI, explained:

I believe the best way for an Indian designer to make it big is by being Indian in their approach. Dior is very French, Armani is truly Italian. I showcase the splendour of Indian textiles and design.

right and far right
'The Baroque Tree',
Wills Lifestyle India
Fashion Week,
Autumn/Winter 2013.

This dedicated approach to the technical development of traditional textiles attained global recognition, but in his view, 'India is shining but not on everyone', which has driven him to ask of his design, 'how do I include deprived weavers, make them stakeholders'? He is passionate about the rates of pay that weavers receive, noting that he can absorb paying them a premium through the higher margins for hand-loom that is crafted for high-end markets. The key is to reinvent traditional hand-loom textiles and crafts in ways that connect them to these markets, but this also means finding ways to overcome the trend-led seasonal nature of the fashion industry by finding new interpretations for the fabrics each year.

I believe the best way for an Indian designer to make it big is by being Indian in their approach. Dior is very French, Armani is truly Italian. I showcase the splendour of Indian textiles and design.

above and right
Dress from Mishra's award-winning collection featuring merino wool and Indian hand-loom textiles.

By 2014 he was showcasing the 'splendour of Indian textiles and design' at the Spring/Summer 2015 Paris fashion week. Here his work with hand-loom and embroideries continued its progression, transforming rural crafts aesthetically and commercially into high fashion.

I am lucky to be born at this time, to be a young Indian at a time when India is growing. In Milan they said to me, yes, you could stay here, be successful driving a Ferrari, but India is the next big thing, you can do a lot there. There is enough inspiration in India to keep me going for many lives.

right and below
'Capsule' collection
for which Mishra
won the 2014
International
Woolmark Prize.
The dress is
embroidered with
fine merino wool
in delicate French
knots. The knots
form interlocking
textured surfaces
that develop on
Mishra's ideas of
tessellation as a
visual metaphor to
express planetary
interdependency
and sustainable
luxury.

Aneeth Arora

opposite
White cotton kedia
by Pero. Photograph:
Tarun Khiwal for
Elle India,
August 2013.

below
Details of the
collection captured
backstage at
Wills Lifestyle
India Fashion
Week, Spring/
Summer 2014.

In a relatively short space of time young designer Aneeth Arora has gained widespread recognition with her label Pero, which means 'to wear' in Marwari, the local language of Rajasthan, North India. Arora's work hones the aesthetic proclivities of hand-loom textiles into a folksy design signature, where layering, loose-fitting silhouettes and characterful detailing define her brand. She studied for her BA at NIFT, and her MA in Textile Design at NID. This was where she began her peripatetic journey documenting craft across India, a journey revealed in her characteristic use of *maheshwari* and

chanderi silks, *telia rumals* from Andhra Pradesh, Bengali cottons, chunky Kumaoni knits from the Himalayas, Madrasi checks and fine *mulmul*. In 2007 she showed her designs as part of the GenNext platform for emerging talent at Lakmé Fashion Week. Her career trajectory has coincided with the emergence of the sustainable and ethical fashion agenda internationally, and in Arora's fresh separates made from traditional Indian textiles assembled with a boho-chic sensibility, it has been perhaps an easier journey for her than some other designers to connect to international markets. A diffusion line, 'Chota Pero' for children, has also been hugely successful in Europe.

Arora speaks the language of craft and ethical fashion through the materiality of small details and whimsical touches such as embroidered hearts and initials. These chime with what sustainability expert Jonathan Chapman has called 'emotionally durable design' where design can heighten emotional attachment to objects, resulting in use-values based on sentiment, longevity and repair.[17] As Rajesh Pratap Singh says, the most organic of cotton is not 'sustainable' if it then enters a fashion system based on trend-led seasons where clothes are quickly discarded for the 'next new thing'. Emotional effect is a huge part of what Arora creates through her clothing, where details and catwalk styling invite entry into her charming, creative universe. The language of childhood play and familial love permeates her collections connected to an emotive and nostalgic vision of craft as a small-scale cottage industry. Her 2013 collection had 'labour of love' hand-embroidered inside the collars, again underscoring the ideal of hand-labour as individual and emotional connectedness, as an idealized response to the perceived alienating effects of mass industrialization.

Arora is very much of the genre of Indian designers who reject form-fitting clothing as an imposition of trend-led

this page
Wills Lifestyle India
Fashion Week,
Spring/Summer
2012.

These little tactile details make the whole experience of wearing Pero more personal and intimate: it's a message to the wearer that we give our undivided attention to each and every piece.

right
'Labour of Love'
Spring/Summer
2014.

overleaf, left page
Wills Lifestyle India
Fashion Week,
Spring/Summer
2014, backstage
before the show;
the hearts on the
small samples show
the work of a group
of women taught
embroidery by Pero.

overleaf, right page
Pero's line for
children 'Chota
Pero', Spring/
Summer 2014, and
backstage shots at
Wills Lifestyle India
Fashion Week.

fashion systems upon the body. Her earliest collections revealed crumpled cottons and chunky knits layered with baggy pants and enveloping scarves. She reflects that at first buyers and media were unsure about her design vision and she was told it would not sell in a fashion market where often design and being 'modern-looking' is equated with Swarovski-encrusted ethnic wear or form-fitting bandage dresses. Arora's clothes chime with anti-fashion ideals of anti-fit and expressive individuality, but she does not achieve this through avant-garde construction techniques. Instead, she looks to the bustling street life in India, drawing inspiration from the way that ordinary people dress, combining this with Western silhouettes.

Arora's strong eye for colour and pattern mixing often defines her Autumn/Winter collections. By contrast, her summer collections frequently focus on cool, fresh all-white ensembles drawing on some of India's finest textile traditions in producing high-thread count, hand-woven muslins and *khadi*.

Arora draws on local styles of dressing, but her interpretation is influenced by Western appropriations of ethnic wear, refracted back through her deft ability to both mirror and synthesize these different strands to her aesthetic. She demonstrates what Niessen describes as a tendency for the dichotomy between fashion and anti-fashion to break down, as ever-proliferating cultural exchange and global flows of images produce references layered upon references: we can see this in Aneeth's referencing of the way that the West has appropriated ethnic styling over the past four decades.[18]

labour of love

opposite, clockwise from top left
Signature draping; signature
clamp-dye techniques using
vegetable dyes, Autumn/Winter
2013; Spring/Summer 2014;
Autumn/Winter 2013.

CellDSGN 11:11

CellDSGN is composed of three designers.
Shani Himanshu and Smita Singh Rathore
graduated from Domus Academy in
Milan in 2003 and then worked for Italian
fashion brands. In 2010 they were joined
by artist-designer Mia Morikawa,
an alumna of Central Saint Martins
in London.

*11.11 sings about using the body as a field of
expression while opening a dialogue on a range
of dualisms such as modernity and tradition:
urban and rural life.*

Their aesthetic is based on deconstructed
silhouettes, printed or distressed
surfaces, exposed seams, raw edges
and drapes that form asymmetrical
shapes inspired by traditional sari-
drapes. As the brand has developed
their design philosophy has also
coalesced around the use of traditional
hand-loom textiles, such as Kala cotton
and indigo denim *khadi*, and craft
techniques including vegetable dyeing,
resist-dye techniques of *bandhani*, *ikat*,
clamp-dying and marbling on crêpe,
all of which create a distinct hand-
painted textile aesthetic. The colour-
resist dyeing they use across their
collections is inspired by the cosmos
and natural structures.

*Seeds promise the formation of future life.
Condensed down into a miniature fragment of
itself, it is the symbol of nature's grand design
and endless power.*

The reclamation and up-cycling of textile
waste is also a central plank of their
design practice. The diffusion line,
'11:11/Reclaimed', breathes new life into
discarded saris, which are re-fashioned
into separates such as tops and baseball
caps. The line also includes woven
iPad sleeves, wallets and bags where
the weft is made from discarded plastic
shopping bags and the warp is organic
cotton. '11:11/Reclaimed' draws on the
Indian concept of *jugaad*, using whatever
is to hand to fashion solutions to everyday
problems. *Jugaad* has resonance with
globally circulating ideas of waste
management and up-cycling and we
see the convergence of these local
and global meanings and practices
in CellDSGN's transformation of
discarded materials.

*All elements come together into a consolidated
look that respects the past, considers the
future and lives in the now.*

As a young brand, they face all the
ubiquitous modern issues of capitalization,
scaling up the supply chain and retail
expansion, especially where lead times
are determined by slow methods of
production at odds with the fast-paced
nature of contemporary supply chains.

*As we supervise directly the hand-making
of the yarn, hand-weaving of our fabric
and dyeing of our thread or garment our
production cycle can reach three months.
In a retailing distribution scheme where
typically a store would reorder at mid-season
and would like the new order to reach within
three weeks, our dynamic does not allow it.
The luxury level we revolve in is essentially
connected with the weavers, spinners, dyers
who are human beings, and as humans and*

above, above right and opposite
11:11 collection made from reclaimed and up-cycled saris.

not machines the speed of production has no shortcuts: 24 hours are required for a day, 30 days in a lunar cycle and three months in a garment creation...

They have started to move towards international expansion which currently generates around 30 per cent of their annual turnover. Currently their core markets remain India and the Middle East.

Within India their dream person to dress would be radical documentary filmmaker Amar Kanwar and internationally:

Freedom fighters and leaders who use their power responsibly and serve their communities with care as well as anyone who values beautiful things.

*The luxury level we revolve in is essentially
connected with the weavers, spinners, dyers who
are human beings, and as humans and not machines
the speed of production has no short cuts.*

Gandhi's Independence movement, which envisioned an economically independent nation based on the hand-spun and hand-woven yarn integral to India's village economy. In Mondal's collection saris in shades of electric blue and russet red were embroidered with delicate kinetic *charkhas*, their energy dancing across the *khadi*, reminding the audience sitting ether side of the catwalk in a heady air of perfume of the grassroots origins of this textile.

Soumitra Mondal

Indian fashion is dominated by highly ornamented bridal and ethnic formal wear, but a corpus of designers create a dynamic dialogue with these aesthetics by using *khadi* at the heart of their creative process and brand positioning. This high-end fashion has to negotiate ideas of craft revival, preservation, heritage and rural livelihoods. As the market for luxury has grown exponentially with international brand expansion into the Indian market, this has also highlighted the role of indigenous textiles and artisanal crafts in the constitution of a uniquely Indian and home-grown luxury market. *Khadi* remains a uniquely Indian textile, promoting sustainable livelihoods and an alternative vision of the relationship between community and market.

opposite
Delicate white *jamdani* in fluid silhouettes. 'Bunon' (Bengali-weaving) Lakmé Fashion Week, Mumbai, Summer/Resort 2012.

right
Khadi sari embroidered with delicate *charkhas*, an enduring emblem of Gandhian philosophy, 'Swadeshi', Lakmé Fashion Week, Mumbai, Autumn/Winter 2009.

Soumitra Mondal, who comes from Kolkata in Bengal, is a quiet force within Indian fashion. In 2002, he created his brand MARG (meaning 'the path' in Bengali). In 2009, he presented a collection called 'Swadeshi' at Lakmé Fashion Week; the collection was named after Mahatma

Mondal has continued to forge a quiet but distinctive voice in Indian fashion. For a time he retreated from fashion shows, but returned when invited to participate in the then newly inaugurated Indian Textile Day at Lakmé Fashion Week in 2012. This gave him the appropriate platform from which to showcase his designs, where craft is never subsumed to fashion, but instead defines it, creating directional craft-based design. His Lakmé 2012 collection 'Bunon' (Bengali for weaving) incorporated saris made from *jamdani*, an exceptionally fine form of Bengali muslin with a supplementary weft which adds the fine detailed patterns. The word *jamdani* is of Persian origin, deriving from *jam* which means flower and *dani* which is a vase or container. The silhouettes are seen on, for instance, saris,

right
Dress made from
delicate layers of
tissue-paper thin
hand-woven
jamdani, Lakmé
Fashion Week,
Mumbai, Winter/
Festive, 2013.

*Working with the immense potential of hand-loom takes
patience and creativity: it is a tough journey and takes much
perseverance from both the designer and craftspeople.
MARG now works with between 350 and 400 highly
skilled artisans.*

below
Sari made
from *jamdani*.

anarkalis, *kurtas* and calf-length pants in shades of white and cream with delicate accents of gold embroidery. White jasmine flowers placed in rows alongside the catwalk and entwined in the models' hair reinforced the ethereal yet strong feminine mood, accompanied by the soundtrack of an old Bengali boatman's tune *Oh Majhe Re* from the 1975 female-ensemble film classic *Khushboo*. These cultural references underscored Mondal's use of *jamdani*.

Jamdani is woven in Bengal and considered to be the finest form of cotton muslin. Its history spans over a thousand years of cultural exchange and Mughal royal patronage. Today, UNESCO has designated it part of India's intangible cultural heritage and it requires the creative vision of philosophical designers such as Mondal to bring it alive for new generations through the frame of the catwalk. For his Lakmé Winter/Festive 2013 collection Mondal displayed his versatility with hand-loom: the ethereal mood of previous collections gave way to a sophisticated dialogue between black hand-loom and the conventions of glamorous evening wear. Silhouettes included a signature cropped blouse,

below
Jamdani weaving has come
under threat and designers
such as Mondal seek to give it
new direction by taking cloth
traditionally woven for saris
and transforming it into tailored
silhouettes, Lakmé Fashion Week,
Mumbai, Winter/Festive 2013.

opposite
Jamdani sari, Lakmé Fashion Week,
Mumbai, Winter/Festive 2013.

rendered as traditional ethic wear when
paired with saris, but honed as part of
linear Western silhouettes when combined
with straight calf-length pants and
covered with semi-transparent hand-
loom *maheshwari* silk *kurtas*. Delicate
black beading accented this collection,
showing how embellishment could be
used to create a mood of subtle luxury.
With MARG, Mondal continues to
navigate a path through Bengal's rich
textile heritage, bringing it alive in
contemporary Indian fashion.

opposite
'Bharua'. Photograph:
Pranoy Sarkar.

below
Kalsi works with women from
impoverished areas in states
such as Bihar and initiates a
collaborative production process
aimed at transforming their
embroidery skills for high
value-added fashion markets.

Swati Kalsi

Swati Kalsi graduated from NIFT, Delhi in
2002 with awards including the best use of
textiles in fashion. She then worked with
Jiyo!, a World Bank-funded project at the
Rajeev Sethi Design Studio. Jiyo! aimed to
reposition traditional artisanal skills in
terms of luxury products, chiming with the
broader turn to heritage and luxury that has
defined craft intervention among Indian
designers and many NGO initiatives over
the past decade. At Jiyo! Kalsi first worked
with groups of women to reinvigorate *sujani*
embroidery skills from Bihar. They were
traditionally used as a form of quilting
to recycle old saris or *dhotis* by piecing
and layering them together with running
stitches which structured the cloth and also
added decoration.

The surface created in sujani, *out of simple
running stitches, moving in transient intensities,
sizes and colours, suggests natural processes
and also reflects the spirit of the creator. This
enticed me to explore textured surfaces in* sujani.

Kalsi has continued to work independently
with the embroiderers, funding innovation
workshops with them herself. The designs
she creates in close collaboration with the
embroiderers take a kinetic, random form,
often seeming to replicate natural rhythms
of elemental forces such as air and water,

overleaf
Kalsi's design work
with the women
results in sujani
with an abstract,
graphic quality.

or the patterns created by the interaction
of nature, plant life and animals: some
embroideries are like water swirling
through a river or birds in flight, while
others appear to trace the intricate
patterns of tree bark.

Many of these patterns are rooted
in cosmological beliefs regarding life-
giving forces, fertility and protection.
Traditionally, *sujani* cloth was used in
gifting and wedding rituals as well as
to wrap newborns in. For many decades
before Jiyo!, NGOs had guided the *sujani*
embroiderers to create motifs based on
pictorial depictions of village life. Kalsi's
innovation was to strip this away and
hone *sujani* embroidery into designs that
express emotion and connectedness free
from figural conventions.

In 2013, Kalsi was invited to show
at the Indian Textile Day at Lakmé
Fashion Week where she won the Lakmé
Heritage Award.

*I was a bit apprehensive about taking textiles
to the ramp since they need to be seen and felt
intimately. Agreeing eventually, I did feel like
taking a chance.*

Now, like many of her contemporaries,
Kalsi is poised between her purist vision
of couture-level luxury, where pieces are
commissioned as one-off creations, or as
very small runs of garments, and the need
to scale-up business to create sustainable
livelihoods both for the artisans she works
with as well as herself.

*The surface created in sujani, out of simple running stitches,
moving in transient intensities, sizes and colours, suggests
natural processes and also reflects the spirit of the creator.
This enticed me to explore textured surfaces in sujani.*

opposite
'Minor'. Photograph: Pranoy Sarkar.

right
'Minor'. Photograph: Pranoy Sarkar.

below
'Bharua'. Photograph: Pranoy Sarkar.

The price of making each such piece is very high. All the works are one-offs, so retail did not feel like an answer since it could not translate well into sales. I feared that making designs more feasible would, however, dilute the value I was trying to bring to the craft. I am still struggling with these issues and am hoping to understand how best these can be addressed.

The whole six yards: continuity and transformations in the Indian sari

opposite

Bagicha sari from the 'Birjoo' collection, 2011. These Varanasi brocade saris from Sanjay Garg's label Raw Mango have patterns inspired by pichwais which depict the Hindu god Krishna.

below

The Gayatri mantra (sacred utterance) is revered by the Vedic tradition. Here we see its personification as a sari-wearing Indian goddess. Courtesy of Professor Christopher Pinney, who was awarded the Padma Shri in 2013 for his distinguished record of work on art, photography and popular visual culture in India.

In essence, the sari is an unstitched length of cloth measuring up to nine, but more typically six yards in length. Putting on an unstitched sari requires skills of pleating and draping in order to secure it to the body. In *Saris of India: Tradition and Beyond*, textile expert Rta Kapur Chishti illustrates over 108 ways of draping a sari. She has worked with weavers for over 30 years to revive traditional weaving styles made from indigenous strains of rain-fed Indian cotton spun on single spool *charkhas* and then finely woven into distinctive regional styles. There is not, however, one kind of sari and today they come in a variety of materials from heavy cotton to the finest muslins (traditionally steeped in starch and crinkled before the hot iron was introduced by the French in 18th-century Bengal). They may have woven patterns using silk threads

wrapped in micro-fine layers of real gold as in the Benaras brocade saris discussed by Crill.[19] They also come in a variety of modern materials including polyester, chiffon and even denim.

Evidence for precursors to the sari is gleaned from ancient art, with Chishti dating sari-weaving back a thousand or more years. Ancient Tamil poetry describes women in exquisite drapery and suggests that a piece of cloth was wrapped around the lower half of the body, while the upper torso was left bare or covered with a separate breast band. Sculptures from the Gupta School (1st–6th centuries AD) show goddesses and dancers, with bare upper torsos, wearing what appears to be a *dhoti* wrap, in the 'fishtail'

right
The Hindu goddess
Lakshmi is seen rising
from a lotus flower
wearing a sari with
gold borders. Artist/
publisher: Raja Ravi
Varma, c. 1890s.
Courtesy of Professor
Christopher Pinney.

far right
Saraswati by
Chorebagan Art
Studio, c. 1880.
Courtesy of Professor
Christopher Pinney.

style, which is tucked and draped between the legs. Many accounts of the sari also connect its form to ancient beliefs regarding the body and cosmos. In the *Natya Shastra*, a treatise describing dance and costume, the navel of the Supreme Being is thought to be the source of life and creativity, hence the practice of leaving the midriff bare when wearing a sari.

It is important to understand that, despite its seeming ubiquity, the sari as we understand it today is a relatively modern invention. The sari's history in the 19th century reflects the dynamic between traditional Indian dress and Western ideas of female behaviour that were introduced under British colonialism. Along with Christian missionaries and the colonial government, the Brahmo Samaj, a Hindu reformist movement closely associated with the family of Nobel Prize-winning poet Rabindranath Tagore, called for the end of repressive practices, such as sati and purdah, against women. Through archival photographs feminist historian Malavika Karlekar has traced how the Brahmo Samaj introduced the reformist attire of a British Victorian-influenced blouse and petticoat over which the sari was draped.[20] This was known as the 'Brahmika' sari. The gentry of rapidly urbanizing 19th-century Bengal, known as the Bhadralok, adopted the Brahmika style, viewing it as progressive and modern, and gradually the style spread among the middle class across India.

In the early 20th century a new mood of Indian nationalism and resistance to colonial rule resulted in cartography where India was anthropomorphized as a great mother. Cultural historian Sumathi Ramaswamy has provided a compelling study of these images of Bharat Mata (Hindi for Mother India) and

right
In the public visual culture of the nationalist movement for independence, India became anthropomorphized as a great mother, Bharat Mata. She is a female personification intimately conflated with the religious symbolism of Hindu goddesses, especially the ferocious Durga. In this image, Bharat Mata proffers a *charkha* to Gandhi, a sword to Subhas Chandra Bose and an Indian flag hung on a trishul to Jawaharlal Nehru. Courtesy of Professor Christopher Pinney.

the maps that were disseminated.[21] The nation and the sari were conflated – in some maps the body of the woman and the drapery of her sari replace the geographical contours of the Indian continent itself. These images became part of a public visual culture that cemented the sari's status as a pan-national garment. In regions where previously women had not traditionally worn saris, its popularity spread, although a multitude of regional ways of draping the sari developed.

right
Detail from a large print 'Swarg Men Bapu' (Gandhi in Heaven), depicting Gandhi's ascent to heaven. The detail shows Bharat Mata weeping. Note how her arms are bent in supplication and the folds of her sari help form an outline that replicates the shape of India. Published by Four Artists, Delhi, c. 1948. Image courtesy of Professor Christopher Pinney.

Raja Ravi Varma (1848–1906), a painter and publisher, published his oil paintings in the European-style; mass-produced chromolithographs depicted Indian goddesses wearing saris, a key way in which the sari's status as a pan-Indian garment proliferated. As art historian Geeta Kapur writes, 'Ravi Varma's paintings...expand into the great shadow-play of popular cinema'.[22] From the early 20th century onwards, cinema images of saris entered into Indian public visual culture. Over time, the sari became caught up in the processes of globalization and, in contrast to hand-loom saris, a burgeoning fashion market means saris may be made from anything from easy-care polyester, light jersey or chiffon.

Traditionally, the way in which a sari is worn can reveal information such as the caste, class or marital status of the wearer, as well as their religion, occupation or regional origin. Yet Aarti Sandhu notes that doctoral research conducted in the 1960s by Justina Singh reveals how educated urban women were turning towards the Nivi style, in contrast to their mothers and grand-mothers who still wore regional styles.[23] In her 1997 book *Saris: An Illustrated Guide to the Indian Art of Draping* cultural anthropologist Chantal Boulanger showed how through various influences the Brahmika style was super-seded by the Nivi style of draping, made popular by famous figures including Maharani Indira Devi of Cooch Behar. Across India, women increasingly gave up local drapes specific to caste, ethnicity or region in favour of the Nivi style, which was viewed as a sign of modernity. In contemporary India, the sari's inimitable associations with traditional Indian womanhood and national patriotism provide fertile ground for preservation or reinvention, adaptation or iconoclasm. Chapter 2 explored designers who translate traditional hand-loom into contemporary urban fashion. While they may adapt weaves traditionally woven for the saris into stitched ethnic and Western silhouettes, many also work within the tradition of hand-woven, unstitched saris. For example, Abraham & Thakore always include innovative sari weaves in their collections and for Spring/Summer 2014, Aneeth Arora created hand-loom polka dot saris.

A different approach altogether revolves around the sari's deconstruction and re-appropriation in terms of Western traditions of cut and construction. In 1999, Tarun Tahiliani was one of the first designers to produce sari-gowns, which are pre-draped and zipped-up rather than unstitched on the body. He reflects: 'The sari embodies the originality and sensuality of the drape – of its fluidity. We've done sari-gowns with corsets, structured and layered drapes.... I think we must live in the present and be fluidly modern.' The sari, although often understood as a traditional item of clothing, has become a key way in which contemporary interpretations, whether based on the ethos of unstitched hand-loom or reinvented as sari-gowns, enable women to express themselves as both rooted in Indian values at the same time as being modern and fashionable. In this sense, while its role in everyday wear is indeed in decline, the sari's place in defining Indian identity is in many ways only amplified as it becomes part of the Indian fashion system, and debates regarding Indian design aesthetics and heritage luxury.

opposite left
Fitted sari-gown by Tarun Tahiliani; in blush pink with Swarovski crystal embellishment.

opposite centre
Model Indrani Dasgupta wears a Banarasi silk sari, part of a collaboration between Abraham & Thakore and sari house Ekaya.

opposite right
The sari is given a tailored and minimalist twist by Arjun Saluja for his collection 'Two Equals One', Wills Lifestyle India Fashion Week, Spring/Summer 2013.

opposite
'Southern Summer' collection, 2014.
Photograph: Shovan Gandhi.

below
Sari with Garg's signature bird
motif, representing his concern for
the declining population of house
sparrows which has been attributed
to interference from mobile phone
masts in India.

Sanjay Garg

In the work of Delhi-based Sanjay Garg the relationship between the revivification of the hand-woven sari and its philosophical role for Indian fashion is evident. Garg's work has a quiet authority that appeals to a surprisingly diverse spectrum of women, from politicians and corporate leaders to actresses and Bollywood's young starlets. Five of his saris are in the permanent collection at the Victoria and Albert Museum in London.

The hand-loom sari is not simply a length of cloth: it has a specific design woven into its body and surface that provides its structure. This structure is made up of the border, body and *pallu* (end of the sari). Eschewing the fashion for heavy ornamentation, Garg advocates minimalism and often reflects that he translates Japanese designer Yohji Yamamoto's dictum that 'Perfection is ugly' into the ethos of hand-woven saris with the idiosyncrasies rendered by the handmade process and, at a metaphorical level, the rejection of globalized trends with their standardized ideals of feminine beauty.

Garg laments the decline in numbers of house sparrows across India, which reports have linked to radiation from mobile phone towers, and a signature motif he uses to decorate his saris are small house sparrows. Above all, he advocates simplicity in his approach to design; yet this does not mean it adheres to the conventions of minimalism. His work may aim to quieten and pare back the decorative patterning of traditional hand-woven saris, but his designs are full of colour and richness. An acidic lime-green is a signature colour for his sari borders, in particular, and other bright colours such as deep pink and marine blue infuse his collections.

Tellingly, Garg advocates his own lexicon for describing the colours of his saris, rooted in Indian culture, traditional medicine and cosmological beliefs about the body, as well as the sari's history of royal patronage. So there is *rani* or *gulabi* pink; *shabarti* orange; yellow made from *haldi* paste, the lime green of *nimbu* and *ferozi* (turquoise).

All of his sari collections are named after aspects of the local cultures where the saris are woven. Although he began by employing four weavers he now employs over 500 on a continuous basis.

below
'Shaher', 2014, a collaboration between
Raw Mango and Hema Shroff Patel.
The collection juxtaposes her busy life
in Mumbai with her peaceful sojourns in
Maheshwar, Madhya Pradesh.

below
'Shaher', 2014.

bottom
With his label Raw Mango, Garg creates saris that blend traditional sari weaving styles with bright colours. Traditional motifs are reworked into patterns that appeal to both sari conoisseurs as well as a younger generation of women.

The sari embodies the originality and sensuality of the drape – of its fluidity.

above left
'Murani' sari for the collection 'Beloved', 2013.

above right
Raw Mango sari. Photograph: Shovan Gandhi, who shot a series of photographs of the collection 'Southern Summer', 2014.

opposite
Photograph: Shovan Gandhi.

You can't just say, don't come tomorrow, and that is the challenge to ensure that my design work creates sustainable livelihoods for the weavers I employ.

In 2014 he showed a line of stitched garments at Lakmé Fashion Week, but under his name. His label Raw Mango remains focused on unstitched saris.

You know that in some parts of India, traditionally they believed that it wasn't right to pierce the cloth with a needle.

Traditional cosmological beliefs regarding cloth, body and cosmos are translated by contemporary designers such as Garg into a particular form of anti-fashion and purist design minimalism in the non-Western fashion context.

Gaurav Gupta

opposite
'Wink of Nyx', Shree
Raj Mahal India
Couture Week, 2014.

right
Lakmé Fashion
Week, Summer/
Resort, Mumbai,
2014. A joint show
by Gupta and
UK-based jewelry
designer Mawi
Keivom.

Delhi-based Gaurav Gupta is one of the most visible designers in terms of his tailoring approach to the sari. With his intricate drapes and pleats, the ways in which the *pallu* is twisted and fixed in sculptural form across the body and the Grecian classicism with which he infuses the contours of the sari's silhouette, his version of the sari is tailored in Western

traditions of cut and construction that create a dynamic conversation between the Indian sari and Western fashion.

Gupta studied at NIFT and Central Saint Martins, London. He won the Future of Couture award at Altaroma Altamoda, Rome Couture Fashion Week, interned with Hussein Chalayan and worked at the studio of Vivienne Westwood.

There is a strong core of fantasy in Gupta's designs which is evident in the sets for his catwalk shows and in his flagship store, in Delhi's luxury mall DLF Emporio, which is styled like a fantasy dungeon with mannequins suspended from the ceiling. Yet he is able to channel this intense creative inspiration into strongly commercial collections popular with affluent brides for *mehndi* ceremonies or as occasion wear for socialites and the younger generation of Bollywood actors.

In Indian art and costume history the influence of 19th-century painter and lithographer Raja Ravi Varma is writ large: his images of archetypal Indian women, as in his painting *Galaxy of Musicians*,

below
Actress Sonam
Kapoor, photograph:
Tejal Patni for *Elle
India*, October 2013.

or of Indian goddesses in flowing saris, reproduced countless times as calendar art, have had immeasurable influence on Indian public visual culture, filtering down across the decades to key vectors of mass communication: cinema, advertising, TV soap operas and fashion. In an interview with journalist Shefalee Vasudev, Gupta explained, 'I can see the Raja Ravi Varma woman in my head, but I try to make a Gaurav Gupta garment for her.'[24] Here then is the link between established tradition and subversive reinvention. If Westwood is renowned for her subversion of historical English and French dress in the British context, then designers such as Gupta undertake a parallel conversation with historic dress forms in India. However, some advocates feel the sari-gown goes against the 'purity' of the sari: one of the key attributes of the traditional six-yard

sari is after all its adaptability to the body of the wearer. The 'fit' is dependent only upon the style and dexterity with which it is draped around the body. With the sari-gown this adaptability is ceded to cut and pre-construction, demanding the body fit into the sari, rather than the other way around. Yet as the introduction to this chapter explored, the sari has undergone many changes in the past two hundred years.

Times have changed, now women are about progressive choices, exposure and attitudes. They have become more experimental and are accepting the new versions of saris. If you look at our work it's very futuristic but at the same time it has costume references from the past and history. My muse is just the mind, a mind that is eager.

This was evident in 'Lightfall', the collection designed for Delhi Couture Week

Times have changed, now women are about progressive choices, exposure and attitudes. They have become more experimental and are accepting the new versions of saris.

left
Actress Shraddha Kapoor
in a sheer sheath that
conceptually references the
essence of the sari's ability to
reveal and conceal the body.
Black bugle beads on net.
Stylist: Vijendra Bhardwaj;
photograph: R. Burman for
GQ India, July 2014.

right and far right
'Wink of Nyx', Shree
Raj Mahal India
Couture Week, 2014.

in 2013. The first design to come onto the catwalk was a sheath, one half of which was covered in tiny glistening black bugle beads that traced a jagged line vertically down the model's body, leaving the other half covered only by the sheerest net. If this seemed antithetical to the sari, one only needs to recall the wet sari scenes that up until recently were a recurring theme of Indian cinema. Wet, transparent saris, made so through convenient narrative devices of monsoon rain or unexpectedly getting caught in thunderstorms, functioned as a proxy for the taboo of nudity. Of course, Gupta was not literally translating the wet sari motif, but drawing on broader themes of seduction, fantasy, danger and taboo, expressed through the play between what is revealed and what is concealed. Across Gupta's collection as a whole this theme of revealing and concealing was reworked with sari drapes pared down to twisted pleats of fabric enclosed around the body with sheer net, also translating to detailing for his ready-to-wear collections that year.

A key signature for Gupta is a sheer bodice, structured through embroidery that replicates the lines and drape of the sari, reducing it down to an abstracted essence of line and form.

I juxtapose Indian embroidery techniques and material like saadi, pitta, zari, nakshee *and multi-dimensional surface ornamentation, organza and lace flowers with drapes, fabric and silhouettes that are almost prophesied for the coming eons. In essence, this collection is about the mystical: mythological characters being looked at from a window of a thousand years from now. It dwells in a space where there is a sense of abandon towards time itself and the only thread connecting this to the ultra-future is light.*

opposite
Bikini sari in polymide and
elastane with Swarovski crystal
and onyx brooch, 'Cruise/Resort'
collection, 2011.

below
'Fontana', Spring/Summer 2014.
The swimwear that season was
inspired by Lucio Fontana, an
Italian painter, who used cuts
and slashed his canvases to
explore spatial depth.

Shivan & Narresh

In the design practice of Shivan & Narresh, the surprising juxtaposition between the bikini and the sari forms a central element in their broader design work of vibrant resort wear.

Indian women have always been comfortable with swimming in public: just think about how women would wear a sari blouse, hook up their saris through their legs and take a dip in the river or at the beach. It's just that swimwear or the bikini is such a Westernized dream that's always been pushed at women here, that there has been an apprehension about wearing a two-piece.

The bikini and the sari: the former a symbol of a Western liberated sexuality since the 1960s, the latter ostensibly a symbol of traditional female identity in India. What happens when these two categories of clothing come together in the bikini-sari? If we understand clothing as central to, even constitutive of, social identity, then what does the bikini-sari tell us about changes in the social fabric of India today?

As the world merges into India and India into the world there is a new aesthetic of modern Indian design. Of course, like anything new and unseen there is an initial reaction of people, wanting to categorize it as Indian, or Western, or even the most abused word in Indian fashion: 'Fusion'!

Our design language is rooted in India. With inventions such as the 'bikini-sari', the idea was to introduce a new silhouette to the world of fashion, yet this creation is local and logical for the lifestyle shift Indians are experiencing today. The path of finding something new has to come from looking within yourself, your culture or society, and that has to be the context of the creation.

Brought up in India, Shivan and Narresh both won scholarships to Italy's Istituto Europeo di Design in Milan. In 2006, at Italy's annual talent search platform Mittelmoda, buyers told them their luxury swimwear with its modest cuts could fill a gap in the market driven by the demographic shift of luxury consumers.

Today, those who bring private yachts to Cannes are Middle Eastern, Russians or Asian and they don't fit into swimwear made with Brazilian or European sizing.

Shivan & Narresh have also caught the wave of domestic luxury tourism in India,

above
Amy Jackson on
location in Goa.
Photograph:
Julian Colston (Salt
Management).

opposite
Bikini sari, 'Mosaic',
Spring/Summer
2012.

with the most affluent of the middle
class holidaying in converted royal
palaces and seaside resorts which have
also become popular destinations for
wedding festivities.

Swim, cruise and resort are three
lifestyles that inform the brand's design
approach. Their lycra bikini-saris (with
pockets for sunscreen and mobile phones)
form part of their resortwear based on
signature colour-blocked separates,
dresses, palazzo pants and shirts colour
blocked in painterly collages of black,
bright jewel hues and pastels. Their ability
for strong storytelling through focused

collections has attracted commercial
collaborations with brands such as
Cointreau, The Taj and Leela Palace hotel
groups and footwear brand Havaianas.

*The demographic for the bikini-sari has been
very intriguing. The versatility of the drape
makes women wear it in a traditional manner
as well as a dress by showing a leg through the
slit. From body-conscious women buying it for
their cruise holidays to young women going for
the bikini-sari for destination weddings and
honeymoons. It's as versatile as the traditional
six-yard sari only made more relevant to
changing, modern India.*

Clothes are not important but what they make you feel and how they can empower you is as important as your existence.

A core objective is to cater for diversity in body types. They reflect that there exists a dearth of technical training and a lack of industry standardization for sizing to produce body and shapewear in India suited to Indian women's body types.

Women in India have been hidden behind layers of clothing in the name of femininity and modesty. The real meaning of modesty and femininity is in virtue of our cultural roots and heritage and has nothing to do with length of hems. Femininity to us is the effortlessly curvaceous Indian body that needs to come out of the closet and women in India need to be proud of their curves and celebrate this freedom. The aim is to free women in India from this complex identity crisis. In decades of promoting Indian heritage and culture, the real identity of women in India seems to have been type-casted and confused. To be seen as a muted figure hidden in a six-yard wonder under a veil is not the expression of an individual. This has to change. Clothes are not important, but what they make you feel and how they can empower you is as important as your existence.

The art of Indian fashion

opposite
Little Shilpa, 'Grey
Matters', Spring/
Summer 2014. The
designer challenges the
boundaries between
fashion and art with
collections that play
with bodily proportion,
gender norms and
ideas of beauty.
Little Shilpa regularly
holds performance
art presentations
at India, Paris and
London fashion
weeks. Photograph:
Prasad Naik.

Art and fashion have a close, if often contested and complex, relationship. Art is frequently perceived as being a more profound creative expression than fashion, a stereotype only perpetuated by the misperception that fashion is mere surface, a frivolous adjunct to the more 'serious' business of art. In turn, the status of art may be claimed to confer value to fashion, especially in the case of couture and luxury. This raises a series of questions about the creative process, its commercial aims and the broader frameworks within which the status of something as 'art' is evaluated.

Fashion's value as art may also exist as a statement of intent to refuse (or at least question) the limitations imposed by a trend-led, 'corporatized' fashion system. Fashion's protagonists insist that at its most elevated expression, as in couture or the work of conceptual designers, fashion is a form of wearable art. Perhaps the best way through these complex debates is provided by Rebecca Arnold, a lecturer in history of dress and textiles at the Courtauld Institute of Art, who states that fashion has its own special concerns, so it is never purely art, craft or industrial design. Fashion incorporates all of these elements and, according to Arnold, should be understood on its own terms, making it all the more fascinating when it intersects with other aspects of art and culture.[25]

Chapter 3 demonstrated the important legacy of art in the symbolism and evolving identity of the sari. More generally, art's relationship to fashion has emerged as a key thread in the evolving identity of contemporary Indian fashion. A key point of reference for this relationship is in the work of Manish Arora. His international reputation as a designer of pop art-influenced fashion bears witness to the vibrancy of India's kaleidoscopic urban streetlife and rapid socio-cultural change over the past two decades, which has resulted in a unique design sensibility among designers such as Arora. Pop art's history in India began in the 1950s with Bhupen Khakhar, of the Baroda School, who brought the so-called 'low culture' of everyday urban life and its aspirations into the frame of Indian art. But the pop art Arora draws on also relates to the oversize graphics of Andy Warhol, who Arora cites as a source of inspiration. Arora's designs mine the melting pot of Indian public

above
Manish Arora, Paris
Fashion Week, Autumn/
Winter 2012. A view
of part of the final line-
up with the completed
graffiti spelling
'Life is Beautiful'
in the background.
Photograph:
Filep Motwary.

visual culture into designs that revel in the idea of India as a spectacle of exuberant colour and ritual.

The other more recent vein of this pop-art appropriation of public visual culture is in the explosion of prints on catwalks in India since around 2011. This younger generation of designers has developed a grammar of playful designs that reinvent markers of Indian daily life for the theatre of high fashion, whether translated into vibrant prints and embroideries, or in the form of recycled materials. Having grown up in a fast-changing society they are steeped in the aesthetics of retro-irony, hence the use of iconic motifs such as bicycles, rickshaws, table-top fans, reading spectacles, cows, moustaches, vintage Bollywood and Indian goddesses to name a few.

This chapter also touches upon incipient aspects of Indian fashion's relationship to art including Indian modernism in painting as well as feminist performance art. Finally, the chapter touches upon the role of artistic practice in allowing designers to use fashion to comment on the fashion system from within, a tradition that goes back to Italian designer Elsa Schiaparelli and which today finds expression in Indian fashion through designers such as Kallol Datta and Little Shilpa.

right
Model Archana Kumar
in a neckpiece from
Manish Arora's design
collaboration with
Amrapali. Stylist: Kshitji
Kankaria; make-up:
Rabgyal; photograph:
Gianluca Santoro.

opposite
In a collection described by Arora
as 'futuristic baroque', metal
embellishments hug the body like
an exoskeleton, Spring/Summer
2011. Stylist: Vandana Sharma;
photograph: Anushka Menon.

Manish Arora

right
'Charmingly
Beautiful' watch
from Arora's design
collaboration with
Swiss brand Swatch.

Manish Arora is one of the most recognized
Indian designers globally with designs
that pulsate energy and colour, irony and
humour. He graduated from NIFT, Delhi,
in 1994, winning the best student award,
and then worked for Rohit Bal, launching
his own label in 1997. He has shown at
Paris Fashion Week since 2007. Now living
in Delhi and Paris, he travels globally
and periodically heads to Goa, absorbing
its hyperbolic culture into his rare
imaginative universe. Arora is known as
the pop-art fashion designer: he cites Andy
Warhol and Roy Lichtenstein as sources of
inspiration. Whether in the vivid energy
of Bollywood posters, goddess stickers on
rickshaws or graphics of street-side stall
signs, Arora has transposed India's public
visual culture into a grammar of icons and
symbols that dance across the surfaces of
his designs.

Arora sees himself as poised at
a particular point in time observing
changes in India under globalization,
and as creating a conversation around
these shifts within the frame of the
catwalk. Often his kaleidoscopic use
of colour and image dominates perceptions
of his designs. It is an image of India and
Indian fashion he at first strategically used
to create highly commercial collaborations
with his own diffusion line that he called

'Fish Fry' and with global brands
including Reebok, Walt Disney, Swarovski,
Nespresso, Barbie, Nivea, Mac and
Swatch. Ongoing international perceptions
of Indian fashion as part of a broader
stereotype of Indian culture mean that
Arora has often been referred to as 'kitsch'
(a term he dislikes) and his work judged
against this broader backdrop of non-
Western in relation to Western fashion.

Yet increasingly Arora seems poised
between different cultures with a distinct
style hard to pinpoint as rooted in any
one time or place. As his career has
progressed, he has collaborated with many
international artists, so that graffiti murals
by New York-based artist Judith Supine
were appliquéd, painted, beaded and
embroidered on Dior 'bar' suits inspired
silhouettes for his Autumn/Winter 2012
Paris show, and Robert Altman's images
from the Jam Festival in Colorado in the
1970s were printed onto the final section
of his Spring/Summer 2012.

Colour and culture have inspired me through the years. I truly believe that life is beautiful and each day lived inspires me. For me each emotion and experience can be translated into a beautiful colour that tells a tale. For instance my Festive/Winter 2013 collection was inspired by the famous Burning Man festival I visited the previous summer. Live, experience and get inspired!

Yet the heady spectacle of Arora's designs often belies a more profound commentary

on Indian society. One of his collections showed men holding hands to provoke recognition of the prejudice against homosexuality in India. In 2013, as horrific cases of violence against women dominated the headlines, public visibility of women's rights was again brought to the fore. These events were on Arora's mind as he conceptualized his first fashion film, *Holi Holy*, directed by Bharat Sikka and starring singer Bishi Bhattacharya

right
Crystal dresses and separates inspired by Hiroshi Nagai whose paintings depict 1980s Miami as a modern-day tropical paradise mixed with references to 1950s surf culture, Paris Fashion Week, Spring/Summer 2011.

opposite
Ready-to-wear Paris Fashion Week, Spring/Summer 2012.

For me it's very important to take India and show it to the world: the world doesn't need another Western designer, what it needs is a modern Indian designer.

above and opposite
Arora collaborated with New York graffiti artist Judith Supine to create print placements on silhouettes inspired by mid-20th-century French couture, Paris Fashion Week, Autumn 2012.

striding around the holy city of Varanasi, goddess-like in one of Arora's futuristic creations. He dedicated the film to the widows of Varanasi who for the first time that year had broken with the custom that widows should stay in a perpetual state of ritual mourning, and played Holi – the Hindu festival of colours. Arora's colours were linked to the humanist emphasis on individual self-expression. The film went on to win Diane Pernet's A Shaded View on Fashion Film (ASVOFF) award.

Arora's earlier tendency towards structured, exaggerated shoulders, which meant he was compared to Thierry Mugler, has given way to more relaxed and fluid silhouettes and luxe separates based on the shapes of relaxed streetwear. In more recent collections his direct transposition of Bollywood imagery and street iconography onto designs has distilled into a vivid palette of neon-sorbet or dark jewel hues and decorative motifs. This detail is rendered with traditional embroidery and beading that Arora says are 'futuristic versions'

of traditional Indian craft techniques. He once commented in an interview with the *Washington Post*, 'There is more to Indian fashion than just being ethnic and traditional.... Everybody is stuck in *zardosi, zardosi, zardosi.*'

As Creative Director for French fashion house Paco Rabanne, he enjoys the challenges presented by new technical developments in materials. In contrast, Arora's recent Paris fashion week collections for his own label have also shown his ability to create highly refined pieces using conventional luxury materials such as leather, silk, hand-beading and ostrich feathers that meet with the expectations of Parisian prêt-à-porter. He is a member of the Fashion Design Council of India and was invited to become a member of the Chambre Syndicale du Prêt à Porter des Couturiers in 2009.

For me it's very important to take India and show it to the world: the world doesn't need another Western designer, what it needs is a modern Indian designer.

of middle-class consumers. But it isn't always the arch aestheticization of the every day, old-fashioned or traditional Bollywood as 'retro' at work: these graphic prints sometimes comment on political change and the shared experience of a generation growing up in the wake of finance minister Manmohan Singh's epoch-changing policies of economic liberalization in the early 1990s. Nowhere is this more evident than in Dev r Nil's Che Guevara sari.

We believe fashion is an important art form through which we can convey messages... not only to show creative influences but also socio-political influences.

Dev r Nil

Around 2011 a new trend of vibrant, playful prints emerged on Indian catwalks, injecting traditional ethnic wear with a fresh, irreverent sensibility. This was archly pop-art print for a cosmopolitan milieu, part of both a global and domestic repackaging of India for a new generation

Dev, a graduate of NIFT, was brought up in Kolkata and Nil was born in Venezuela, but grew up partly in India and Australia. They met by chance when Nil was visiting India and formed an instant bond, quickly forming a design partnership where Dev

left
Taxi print suit, Wills Lifestyle India Fashion Week, Spring/ Summer 2013.

right
The 'Change of Guard' collection included pop art images of Che Guevara's motorcycle.

opposite
Che Guevara print sari, part of the 'Change of Guard' collection for Wills Lifestyle India Fashion Week, Spring/ Summer 2011.

A vivid image we also spoke about was heartbreak. The broken wire print references those silly yet deeply felt teenage heartbreaks. The print was inspired from the broken string of a badminton racket which symbolized unfulfilled memories of love and desire.

opposite, above right and below right
'Lost and Found', Spring/Summer 2013. Innovative details in the print include a broken line. The designs symbolize the broken string of a badminton racket, a metaphor for childhood games and first heartbreaks.

takes care of the creative process while Nil manages the business, employing a workforce of 240 people. They invest in training to create employment, particularly among marginalized groups such as the transgender community. In 2014, with a new 4000-sq-ft Kolkata-based flagship store, they celebrated ten years as a brand. They are based in Kolkata, once a centre of British colonial rule, famous for its intellectual and artistic heritage, and latterly as a centre of communist Marxist rule, which provides the rich socio-political background to their designs. In 2011, they developed on their previous use of print with a collection called 'A Change of Guard'.

The collection commented on upcoming elections amid the political ferment occurring at the time in Bengal, India's fourth most populous state (with a population of 91 million), where the world's longest-running democratically elected Communist party had held power for over 30 years. Yet under this government west Bengal had spun into economic decline and the Bengal education system had become dominated by a cadre network banning English in schools, ironically serving to marginalize the poorest even further from a burgeoning service and IT sector where English is key. This cadre network was also believed to have resorted

above
Autumn/Winter 2013.

to voter intimidation and vote rigging. The public visual culture of Bengal was dominated by icons of the global Communist left such as hammer and sickles painted on buildings, roads named after Karl Marx and statues of Lenin.

We wanted to work with something very close to our heart...at that moment Bengal was going through immense upheaval, the ruling Communist party of 33 years was on the verge of collapse, people were ready for change. Our collection used images of Che Guevara. We used images of Che and his motorbike to convey the

message of imminent change sweeping through Bengal. It was a deliberate irony that we used a leftist/Marxist icon (Che Guevara) to talk about the impending change of Marxist political rule in Bengal.... We started with various kinds of tie dye, ombre and dip dyeing techniques, slowly moving on to block print (our 'Sixty' collection in 2008) and batik. We have in-house screenmaking and printing facilities. We don't use digital printing as we don't find it has the clarity or the soul required for a print. But what has become our main forte nowadays is to combine printing with thread texturing, thus blurring the lines between prints and embroideries as a texture.

left, right and below
'Lost and Found', Spring/Summer 2013. The collection included a heart print made from Dev r Nil's own overlapping thumb prints (above left and right).

Their Spring/Summer 2013 collection 'Lost and Found' continued to use print in thought-provoking and profoundly autobiographical form.

We were talking about the childhood memories which we yearn for as we start growing older. The nostalgia for those free-spirited days and playfulness. A vivid image we also spoke about was heartbreak. The broken wire print references those silly yet deeply felt teenage heartbreaks. The print was inspired from the broken string of a badminton racket which symbolized unfulfilled memories of love and desire. From the same 'Lost and Found' collection the thumb print [Dev and Nil's thumbs put together] speaks of those little love stories from childhood in a very playful tone. But the heart-shaped thumb print also personalizes a story and our work. It leaves a personal touch in our art work.

Little Shilpa

Little Shilpa is the nickname of Shilpa Chavan, a Mumbai-based hat designer. With her surreal and highly conceptual millinery, Little Shilpa's designs defy the boundaries between fashion and art; the use of found objects and recycling are passions that she pursues with a dedicated attention to the sculptural possibilities of materials as unexpected as rubber flip-flops or pieces of vintage saris. She also excels at the subversive use of consumer goods which now abound in cheap street markets across India. For example, her 2009 collection 'Headonism' at London Fashion Week used plastic bangles. Traditionally associated with femininity and worn clustered on the arms of a bride in the first

below and opposite
'Hedonism', 2009.
The headpiece
(below) is made
from overlapped
padded bras.

weeks after her marriage or as a fashion statement, they extended like precarious antennae on one of Little Shilpa's hats, the illusion of her torso-less head set on top of a backdrop of kitsch domestic paraphernalia. Another hat was made from overlapping black bras folded over the model's head like an exotic turban, red glitter lips replacing her own in an extenuated gesture of seductive femininity. Chavan's provocative millinery can be contextualized as part of the visual interpretation of gender issues by feminist artists such as Chitra Ganesh, Bharti Kher and Pushpamala N, whose work subverts markers of conventional female identity; these artists, writes art critic Zehra Jumabhoy, share a visual language of

'dirty-pretty things to address male-female concerns'.[26]

Her collection 'Battle Royale', shown at Lakmé Fashion Week in 2010, had a military theme, punctuated with humour and an ingenious ability to express darker, brooding themes through beauty and the absurd, disquieting juxtapositions. Models dressed in khaki military uniforms wore headpieces including one where toy helicopters 'flew' around the woman's head in lilliputian proportions, serving to bestow her with a nation-like scale. This recalled the public visual culture of Indian nationalism that sought to turn the geographic landscape into an anthropomorphic body in the name of

opposite
'Battle Royale',
Autumn/Winter 2009.

right
Perspex accessories
from 'Rainbow Totem',
Autumn/Winter 2010.

below right
'Grey Matters',
Spring/Summer 2014.

pan-Indian nation building and often used images of goddesses as the all-Indian mother Bharat Mata. Art historian Sumathi Ramaswamy discusses how Bharat Mata's body replaced the geographic contours of the Indian map, 'this patriotic visual labour turned India into a homeland to live and to die for'.[27] 'Battle Royale' was Chavan's commentary on the role of pomp, ritual and individual sacrifice in the name of nation building.

The inspiration for this collection has been our history and our current relationship with war... from the times of our maharajas to the present day and also the future...it is something that we live with every day. This is obvious in the use vintage medallions, military regalia, gold crowns and brocade fabric. It is a juxtaposition of two worlds that collided in India at the time of the Raj.

Little Shilpa's working methods rely on individual studio craft production, limiting the expansion of her business, but she prefers the process of making each unique piece herself. 'Fleurs du Mal', 2011, which used hats decorated with flowers like halos around the models' heads, was inspired by 19th-century French poet Charles Baudelaire, whose poem *Les Fleurs du mal* expressed themes of decadence and decay against the backdrop of political and cultural change when medieval parts of Paris were demolished to make way for modern city planning. These influences

below
'Cranes Flying across the Sky', Lakmé Fashion Week, Mumbai, Autumn/Winter 2011.

opposite
'Fleurs du Mal', Autumn/Winter 2011.

were channelled through Little Shilpa's play on opposites of blooming fecundity and death and stagnation. The models were given a ghostly beauty, dressed in white, a colour traditionally associated with mourning in India. Flowers printed on perspex circled around the models' heads and hung from their necks. Fragments of vintage saris worn by Little Shilpa's mother were encased between slices of perspex, hung around the neck like amulets or *memento mori*. There was a sense of intense nostalgia for the passing of so much that was familiar in what she recalls as her middle-class childhood, memories sharpened against a sense of watching time slip away more rapidly in the wake of the massive changes India has undergone as a society embracing both consumer culture and globalization at an accelerated pace since the 1990s. The small details contained within the arresting theatre of Little Shilpa's creations invite us to reflect on these broader themes. Often her hats, assembled from the discarded detritus of everyday urban life, are metaphorical for urban issues of pollution and anonymity. In her work detritus is transformed into beauty with an often dark, foreboding mood.

She trained at Central Saint Martins in London and then with high-society milliner Philip Treacy learning the technical skills of hatmaking and the business side of running a fashion label. Although Lakmé had never had catwalk collections dedicated to accessories, they agreed to do so after Little Shilpa presented them with a proposal for a runway show. She emphasizes that it's not that the Indian market isn't ready for these kind of things, simply that platforms are limited.

She embodies the idea that fashion should be about the expression of individuality. But since India remains a very new market for millinery in general, and she occupies the space in fashion that overlaps closely with the idea of art: perhaps we could also call it fashion for fashion's sake. Little Shilpa is nonetheless an influencer whose flights of creative inspiration are awaited each season by fashion media and designers. It is a space she is happy to occupy, exhibiting in international galleries, presenting regularly at London Fashion Week's talent platforms and from time to time accepting commercial sponsors that allow her to stage memorable shows.

I have always been very inspired by Indian gods and goddesses. Their crowns or headpieces lend a sense of ambiguity and omnipotence to the wearer. This is perhaps my earliest inspiration that led me to become a milliner.

opposite
'A Fine Balance' collection,
Autumn/Winter 2013. Inthis collection
Khandwala was concerned with
nonconformist individuality and
sought to express a mood of feminine
strength in her work.

below
Autumn/Winter 2013 line-up for finale
at Lakmé Fashion Week, Mumbai.

find clothing that was 'mature, simple but stylish and still comfortable'.

I think too many women struggle with body image. So I make a conscious effort when I design to keep our clothes comfortable. That drives a lot of my subsequent choices in terms of silhouettes and construction. I keep the silhouettes purposefully long, because for the rest of us mortals (that are not represented on runways) length can make us looker taller, slimmer, even if it is just an illusion. I favour pleats and drapes to allow the clothes to float around the body – rather than trying to squeeze our bodies into clothes that are too tight, too short, and our self esteem into a heap of Spanx. Also I am relentless in my pursuit of proportions. I think we do ourselves a great disservice by picking clothes that are not well proportioned. I like to think making a garment is a bit architectural in a way.

Payal Khandwala

Payal Khandwala is a designer whose creative process blurs the boundaries between art and fashion. Her fashion designs do not defy conventions in any extreme sense, although she could be said to be 'anti-fashion' in her adherence to fluid drapes and silhouettes designed to adjust to the body and individuality of the wearer. The 'art' in her fashion is in the dialogue it holds with the figurative and abstract painted canvases she creates. When asked what inspires her to create, without hesitation she replies 'daughter, both figural and literal'. We can understand the nurturing dynamic inherent in this source of inspiration through the two creative forms she works with, abstract and corporeal: flat canvases and real bodies.

What is immediately striking about her paintings and her fashion designs is the dynamic between rich jewel hues and earthy tones. Her Lakmé Summer Resort collection 'Play' cited inspiration from abstract expressionist painter Mark Rothko. In her abstract paintings, in particular, Khandwala is concerned with the way that both form and colour can visually represent as well as evoke feelings, and the ways that paintings can construct a physical reality for intangible emotions. She says she began designing (launching her label in 2012) because she could never

Born in Mumbai, Khandwala received an art scholarship in 1990 and graduated from SNDT, Mumbai. From 1995 she spent several years in New York at the Parsons The New School for Design, graduating with a BFA in Fine Arts and Illustration. Her paintings can be found in galleries and private collections internationally. Her fashion designs explore the tensions between masculine and feminine elements, expressed in the play of drape and

left
Lakmé Fashion Week, Mumbai, Spring/Summer 2014.

below
Mixed media on canvas, 2005, juxtaposed with 'A Fine Balance', Lakmé Fashion Week, Mumbai, Autumn/Winter 2013.

opposite above
Oil on canvas, 2006, juxtaposed with chartreuse silk dress from 'A Perfect Fit', Lakmé Fashion Week, Mumbai, Spring/Summer 2014.

opposite below
Oil on canvas, 2007, juxtaposed with white shirt and Benares silk skirt from 'A Perfect Fit', Spring/Summer 2014 and a shirt and sari from 'A Fine Balance', Autumn/Winter 2013.

I always found it impossible to categorize my art: it's the same with my clothes. I hope that it's in some category that transcends geographical boundaries and cultural references.

below
Lakmé Fashion Week,
Mumbai, Spring/Summer
2014.

right and opposite left
Rich colours, line and
strong composition
are evident in both
Khandwala's design and
her artistic practice.

opposite right
'Play', Summer/Resort 2012.

structure. Line, composition and
colour across both her abstract and
figurative oil paintings are strong and
focused, and we can see the creative
transformation of these principles into
her designs, where the dynamic tensions
created by linear draping, asymmetrical,
geometric shapes and a keen eye for
proportion in the silhouette constitute
her design signature.

*Colour is integral to my vocabulary across both
disciplines, and definitely is a key link between
the two.... My preoccupation with the human
form, with line, shape, proportions and colour
tend to spill over into both. It's sort of an
on-going dialogue.*

Khandwala's use, in particular, of lustrous hand-woven silk by sari weavers in Bengal lends her designs a sensuality and richness that, combined with the way the fabric moves fluidly across the body, results in designs that emphasize femininity but in a subtle, intellectual way. Colour is her *métier* whether rendered on flat canvas or the 'canvas' of the body. Perhaps the key difference in this process of creative translation between art and fashion is the concession she makes to practicality in the latter, always keeping in mind that the clothing she creates should

... still allow you to sit and walk and breathe. I try to keep things fuss-free. I find it satisfying to *take flat pieces of fabric with simple beginnings – squares, rectangles, circles – and slit, fold, stitch them into garments, with minimal invasive tailoring. I love building shapes on my dummy.*

Her own work can be understood as part of a long continuity of Indian artistic practice that has sought to explore international art forms through Indian mythology, culture and iconography. She often speaks of her designs having an 'Indian soul' but an international appeal. When asked whether she identifies with terms such as 'Indo-Western, ethnic or boho-chic', she responds,

I always found it impossible to categorize my art: it's the same with my clothes.

Kallol Datta 1955

near right
Signature circular-cut silhouettes have defined Datta's work since early on in his career, Lakmé Fashion Week, Mumbai, Autumn/Winter 2009.

far right
Circular cutting techniques and deconstructed tailoring are methods Datta uses to create silhouettes that are at once voluminous and sinuous. Image by Surbhi Sethi, www.headtilt.in.

opposite
'XOXO', Mercedes-Benz Fashion Week, Berlin, Autumn/Winter 2012.
The themes of heartbreak are explored through deconstructed garments.

Kolkata-based designer Kallol Datta proffers a brooding, cerebral intervention with his anti-fit, conceptual approach to design. He challenges conventional meanings of fashion, especially its relationship to the body, an increasingly significant issue in India as globalized ideals of body shape, weight and beauty become prevalent. He advocates fashion as individual expression, emphasizing that his designs appeal to 'women who do not use their sexual energy as their main currency for attraction'. Indeed his designs demand conscious engagement with voluminous silhouettes produced by circular cutting techniques, their asymmetrical shapes, off-beat prints and the surface interruptions of drapes and pleats. His design identity is global while looking inward into Indian society. Although he was born in India, he spent much of his childhood in the UAE and Bahrain. He remembers 'billowing silhouettes in black and white' set against desert landscapes. He is also inspired by Japanese fashion, art and film, so overall his designs represent a fascinating alchemy of non-Western fashion influences.

My clothes go straight from runway to rack without any modifications, without any compromises. My relationship with my clients is to the point. I make no excuses for them and at the same time I need to invest time in educating them that clothes like that of my label exist.

opposite left
'XOXO', Mercedes Benz Fashion Week, Berlin, Autumn/Winter 2012.

opposite right
'This is not a Garment', 'XOXO', Wills Lifestyle India Fashion Week, Autumn/Winter 2012.

below
'Abandon', Project 88 Gallery, Mumbai, Autumn/Winter 2013. The model is constricted to the chair, a monkey attached by a chain echoes her sense of confinement and symbolizes Datta's ambivalence towards the fashion industry.

Despite his non-commercial approach, Datta's designs propose a highly individualistic way of dressing that has attracted him much attention in the fashion industry. As part of its new focus on young talent, Lakmé Fashion Week invited him to show (along with Pankaj & Nidhi) for its Winter/Festive 2012 edition, featuring Bollywood actress Kareena Kapoor. Datta presented 'Monochrome' with signature oversize silhouettes and a print based on foetuses and snails. He is philosophical about the criticism this attracted from those who expected a dazzling cocktail gown.

In India, the designer who is 'awarded' the finale has to have a larger-than-life, grand show. I am not that designer.... I know that I am the fish bait in the food chain vis-à-vis the fashion industry. I am very comfortable with this positioning.

He studied fashion at NIFT, Kolkata and womenswear at Central Saint Martins, London, launching his label Kallol

Datta 1955 in 2007 (1955 refers to the year his mother was born). His inspirations include Spanish artist Salvador Dalí; the Surrealists' concern with death and decay permeate his own work.

The grotesque, whether blood, bones, internal organs or body parts withered with age, has formed part of the conceptual basis of Datta's collections. An established tradition sees artists using carnival and grotesque corporeal practices as tactics to unsettle power. Journalist Chinki Sinha has written about a further influence in this vein – the early 20th-century Japanese artistic movement Ero Guro Nansensu (Eroguro), which explored eroticism, sexual corruption and decadence.[28] Social historians have contextualized Eroguro as part of the turbulent era of political and social change in 1920s Japan, but Eroguro's social context has often been overlooked in its reception by the West, where its graphic depictions of blood, mutilation and violence are foregrounded and caricatured.

For lack of a better word, my prints were called 'quirky' and 'experimental'. Hence the declaration of the quirky print being dead for me at least. I still use print but the storytelling is stronger now that I use digital prints on fabric with the 'assemblage' method.

below left
'Selfie sari' printed
with images of
the designer in
a knowing parody
of the cult of
creative genius that
surrounds many
fashion designers.
Wills Lifestyle India
Fashion Week,
Autumn/Winter 2014.

below centre
Red sari, Wills
Lifestyle India
Fashion Week,
Autumn/Winter 2014.

below right
Chevron print,
Wills Lifestyle India
Fashion Week,
Autumn/Winter 2014.

This chimed with Datta's own sense of frustration at how his concepts were 'lost in translation' and he called his Spring/Summer 2013 collection 'Grotesque Nonsense'. He was particularly aggrieved by how media coverage of his prints described them as 'quirky'. Indeed, Datta was one of the designers whose striking prints became part of a broader trend on Indian catwalks, yet he felt this pigeon-holed him, with cut and construction overshadowed by media fanfare that sensationalized or made whimsy of his graphic prints. He took a decisive step for Autumn/Winter 2013 and rather than holding a show during fashion week, he held a private view of his collection called 'Abandon' at Mumbai's Project 88 Gallery. The presentation juxtaposed garments hung alongside statements, objects and photographs in a gallery setting that Datta curated, hoping to create meaningful discussion around his work. A framed print with the words 'Quirky Prints' was draped with a black garland as a symbol of mourning. Another exhibit featured a photograph of a seated model with her arms pinned to the chair and a monkey on her lap tethered by a chain; across the print Datta had agitatedly scrawled 'Quirky Fucking Print'.

For lack of a better word, my prints were called 'quirky' and 'experimental'. Hence the declaration of the quirky print being dead for me at least. I still use print but the storytelling is stronger now that I use digital prints on fabric with the 'assemblage' method.

Datta has continued to use seemingly grotesque imagery in his prints. A collection labelled 'XOXO', Autumn/

right
Detail of 'Crop top
shapewear peplum
cut-out' dress, Wills
Lifestyle India
Fashion Week,
Autumn/Winter 2014.
Photograph:
Surbhi Sethi,
www. headtilt.in.

far right
For Wills Lifestyle
India Fashion
Week, Autumn/
Winter 2014, Datta
produced a series of
prints known as the
'Bloodsong' series
based on his artist's
residency at Koj.
Photograph:
Surbhi Sethi,
www.headtilt.in.

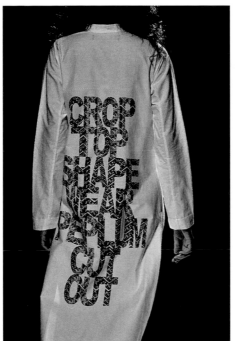

Winter 2012, shown at Mercedes-Benz Fashion Week in Berlin, was inspired by a recurring dream of a grey-haired woman conducting autopsies of people who had died of heartbreak. The internal organs of the body are most obviously metaphorical in the case of the heart, the biological organ connected by poets and artists to love. Deconstructed garments included hoods sewn to the front of dresses and a cape with its bottom half fastened through a regimented row of buttons that could be done or undone.

For Wills Lifestyle India Fashion Week, Autumn/Winter 2014, he included a sari called 'Bloodsong' and images transposed from his 2013 residency at the Khoj International Artists' Association, Delhi, where he had created an installation using self-portraits and suspended phials slowly dropping blood (some of it his own) into glass jars in a chilled room reminiscent of a pathology lab. Datta spoke of his fascination with how thoughts and emotions can be expressed through material form.

In a highly satirical gesture the collection also included a signature voluminous dress, the latest trends spelled out on the back: 'Crop top. Shape wear. Peplum. Cut out.'

I do feel safer and more secure when in residence at an art foundation. It is, however, not so different from the fashion industry, when I am invited to showcase at an art fair. At the end of the day my work has to bring forth into conversation: humans, their insecurities, and the symptoms, which accompany such fears like self-worth, loathing and paranoia. When I am forced to face the same, the way in which they're brought forth, motivates the not so happy part in me. And that makes me happy. It is not a positive or a negative. It is but a basic human character trait.

Designing the boundaries of Indian fashion

opposite
Pankaj & Nidhi won
the Indian round of the
International Woolmark
Prize, 2012. A dress
from the prize-wining
collection featuring
embroidered wool
crewelwork.

As art historian Adam Geczy writes in *Fashion and Orientalism: Dress, Textiles and Culture from the 17th to the 21st Century*:

> *The fate of clothing in the broad reach of the many countries that at one time were associated with the Orient has been either to re-adopt and re-enact tradition as a form of resistance, and as a mainstay of its own cultural norms, or to meld casually into the normalizing fog of the global environment. Binaries are often good places to start a critical discussion, but the issue is a lot more complex with numerous coordinates.*[29]

This chapter extends this discussion further through the exploration of designers whose work represents an on-going and often ground-breaking dialogue with the history and socio-cultural context of Indian fashion, as well as conversations with other non-Western fashion centres. The ways these designers work forms part of the broader conversation with the commercially dominant aesthetics of the bridal industry and, again, represents the relatively niche but growing arena of design-led Indian fashion that seeks to find fresh expression free from the conventions of Bollywood and bridal-influenced style. More than ever, their work highlights the limiting nature of conventional binaries when it comes to understanding Indian fashion. In relation to this, the chapter draws out the following key themes: the meanings of anti-fashion in the Indian context; the role of non-Western fashion markets, especially in Western Asia, in influencing the direction of Indian fashion; the synthesis of foreign cultural inspirations; and the changing role of women in Indian society, which many fashion designers address though reinterpreted traditional design that comments on issues of gender and power.

Anti-fashion

In one sense, being and doing anti-fashion represents the resistance to forms of dress brought about historically through colonialism, and in contemporary times through globalization. Traditional clothing is celebrated as a form of oppositional dress, denoting national identity and authentic values. Yet as we

right
Amit Aggarwal, Couture
collection, reinvented
bridal *lehengas* in
futuristic terms with
metal caging and
carapaces, Lakmé
Fashion Week, Winter/
Festive 2013.

far right
Arjun Saluja,
deconstructed, distressed
leather jacket contrasted
with Pakistani silk *khais
dhoti* pants, 'Between
Time', Wills Lifestyle
India Fashion Week,
Autumn/Winter 2014.
Photograph: Surbhi
Sethi, www.headtilt.in.

have seen in the case of many designers in this book, there is another dimension to the idea of being 'anti-fashion' that exists within the Indian context and cannot be so easily understood in terms of the binaries of East and West. Where the bridal market and Bollywood bling dominate the aesthetics and economy of Indian fashion, we have seen how certain designers hinge their design aesthetic, creative process and brand philosophy on working with pared-down traditional silhouettes and minimally ornamented hand-loom, creating a form of 'anti-fashion' dialogue within the Indian context itself.

Some Indian designers take inspiration from a pan-Asian movement of anti-fashion, notably the Japanese designers who gained enormous recognition in the 1990s. In 2014, the influence of Japanese designers such as Yohji Yamamoto and Issey Miyake was again clearly evident across European designer collections in Paris and Milan, and a new minimalism that undoubtedly had influences emanating from these designers had, in certain adapted forms, filtered down to European high streets. Their legacy resonates across catwalks today in Paris and London and also in India, challenging the East–West fashion dichotomy and at a more profound level ideas of construction, fit and silhouette. But what about these influences and their particular meanings and appropriations in the Indian context? Arjun Saluja represents this complex and fascinating dialogue in his cerebral, non-conformist work.

But does resistance to dominant modes of Indian fashion necessarily mean minimalism? Ornamentation and richly embellished clothing is also being

below
Eina Ahluwalia,
'Heart of Gold' brooch
from 'Forgotten Jewel'.

created with aesthetics that depart from the conventions of bridal wear. We have seen, for example, how Anamika Khanna infuses traditional ethnic wear with new ideas of ornamentation and bridal wear, and some designers resist categorization altogether through cohesive blends of techniques, ornamentation and inspiration from different cultures. Pankaj & Nidhi were trained under veteran designer Rohit Bal and they now work in what might be called a new tradition of Indian couture, which is also in tune with the development of 'demi-couture' by European designers such as Mary Katrantzou, Christopher Kane and Matthew Williamson. Demi-couture brings together the convenience of ready-to-wear with the craft details of the atelier. With its tradition of intricate embroidery techniques, Indian fashion is well placed to create its own version of demi-couture. Pankaj & Nidhi's work points to how contemporary Indian fashion outside of the aesthetics of the bridal market does not necessarily have to mean minimalism, but instead a fresh way of approaching highly ornamented clothing. For European designers their markets are increasingly influenced by consumers in non-Western countries such as China, Japan and Dubai. The demands of these consumers are also influencing new models of luxury ready-to-wear, and it is important to see Pankaj & Nidhi's work within this broader global context as well as the domestic Indian one: not least given the importance of Dubai and other Western Asian markets to Indian fashion designers.

What Pankaj & Nidhi also represent is the synthesis of aesthetic influences that blur notions of culture, history and nation. Another key designer in this vein, Amit Aggarwal, is known for his designs that build organic shapes around the body. While he is regularly worn by Bollywood stars on magazine covers and at events, it is in Western Asian markets that he has found the greatest commercial success. This again highlights the importance of non-Western fashion centres in forging a new direction for luxury fashion as a global phenomenon. This chapter also looks at the work of Eina Ahluwalia whose jewelry designs chime with the New Jewellery Movement of the 1970s. She has melded many of the core ideas of this movement into her signature pieces that challenge conventional ways of thinking about and wearing jewelry.

From the binary categories of Indo-Western, Anglo-Indian or ethnic-chic, and in the long trajectory of fusion and cross-cultural influence, is something qualitatively new being created in the sphere of non-Western fashion? This chapter seeks to explore this question through the design practice of some of India's most innovative designers, known for their mix of Eastern and Western influences as well as the dialogue they create between 'Eastern' forms of fashion themselves.

opposite
Distressed, deconstructed leather jackets
contrast with the heavy drapes of Pakistani
silk Khais, 'Between Time', Wills Lifestyle
India Fashion Week, Autumn/Winter 2014.
Photograph: Surbhi Sethi, www.headtilt.in.

Arjun Saluja

right
Garments that stand
away from the body
emphasize Saluja's
focus on clothes
as experiments
with identity and
individuality.
Photograph:
Surbhi Sethi,
www.headtilt.in.

Arjun Saluja's designs represent a quiet yet radical vision of fashion that acts as both a barometer of, and a provocation to, wider societal change. His silhouettes balance structure and volume, resulting in shapes that sometimes cocoon the body, wrapping it in swathes of fabric, or structure the body with rigid lines. His designs are androgynous, cerebral, full of the unexpected and do not conform, but instead point towards new ways of seeing and existing through Indian fashion. His label 'Rishta', which means 'relationship' in Hindi, is an ode to his mother who was also a designer.

I didn't want to become a designer, I wanted to work in theatre, music or the arts, yet somehow I became a fashion designer. It wasn't like a choice: it was almost inevitable. I don't like to put my fashion design in a box and say it's just fashion: theatre, dance, music and art are all forms of expression that influence me and that I express through my design work. Fashion is simply another art form in this sense.

Androgyny is at the heart of his work, an understanding of which Saluja states can be refined through the ancient concept of Ardhnarishwar (Sanskrit for half-male, half-female), rooted in Vedic creation myths in the form of the androgynous cosmic man Purusha. The *Brihadaranyaka Upanishad* says that Purusha splits himself into two parts, male and female, and the two halves then go on to produce all life.

My designs are not intended to have any gender, they can be worn by a man or by a woman; they express a state of mind. It's how you play with your identity, how you express it through clothing, and how clothing shapes and expresses identity.

This design philosophy was expressed in Saluja's work at Wills Lifestyle India Fashion Week, Spring/Summer 2013, where he took inspiration from Jeet Thayil's novel *Narcopolis*. The story is about a eunuch called Dimple and life in the underbelly and opium dens of what was then Bombay. The opium den brings together Hindus, Sikhs and Muslims in a languorous haze of drug-induced torpor, a haze broken by the influx of street heroin and the communal violence that explodes on the streets in the 1990s. Dimple searches to find beauty in a conflicted world of social conventions underneath which seethes corruption and

I think about the mind when I design my clothing, what kind of mind the woman I design for has, strong, independent; they are nomadic individuals, not bound by conventions.

opposite
Cocoon coat from
'No Ground Beneath
my Feet', Autumn/
Winter 2012.
Photograph: Karel
Losenicky for *Harper's
Bazaar India*,
September 2012.

below
'Aik', Wills Lifestyle India Fashion Week, Autumn/Winter 2013.

hypocrisy. Clothing, with its potential to transform identity and blur genders, allows her to seek to transform her world, moving between religions, genders, states of reality, time and social roles. Saluja's collection expressed Dimple's search for a single truth through opposing facets in silhouettes that explored her personality and prints based on Islamic architectural motifs that referenced her environment.

I have a lot of strong female influences in my life, a lot of very individual, strong female friends who work in cinema, the arts, law. They've led their lives very much on their own terms, not always an easy thing to do in India, where it can still be tough for an independent modern woman. I think about the mind when I design my clothing, what kind of mind the woman I design for has, strong, independent; they are nomadic individuals, not bound by conventions.

Saluja is also concerned with transcending the binaries so often used to categorize silhouettes as Indian or Western or the binaries implicit in fusion concepts such as ethnic-chic or Indo-Western. There is freshness in the way he blends influences that defy these categorizations. When Saluja introduces traditional ethnic clothing into his designs there is a sense of questioning and deconstruction. For Wills Lifestyle India Fashion Week, Autumn/Winter 2014, he created a dynamic through the juxtaposition of line and drape emphasized through cut and materials.

right
Deconstructed
leather jacket,
Wills Lifestyle India
Fashion Week,
Autumn/Winter
2014. Photograph:
Surbhi Sethi,
www.headtilt.in.

far right
Saluja's signature
concern with
structure versus
drape was used to
explore the theme
of migrancy where
'the labourer's
flowing existence
ironically constructs
stability'. Burnt
sequins on the lapel
symbolize dreams
deconstructed into
reality. 'No Ground
Beneath my Feet',
Wills Lifestyle India
Fashion Week,
Autumn/Winter 2012.

Pants based on the *dhoti* drape were
tailored to give them a high-fashion
aesthetic and were worn with distressed
leather jackets where misplaced zippers
traced arching lines across the torso;
a rich silk sari suggested the burnish
of antique silver and was worn with a
cropped distressed leather vest; shoulders
were either boxy or cocoon-shaped, and
silhouettes were balanced between the
fitted and draped but remain streamlined
throughout so that volume was sinuous
and not bulky. Again Islamic culture
influenced the decorative elements of his
collections – in this case, the Pakistani
Khais technique using jacquard and
heavy silk drapes. He is sanguine about
the question of national identity in
fashion design.

*As in France, Italy or London, there is a specific
history and this influences the design process
and the silhouettes, so it's the same in India.
But cultural influences should never result
in costume, they should never be interpreted
too literally.*

In Saluja's work garments swathe the body,
moving sensually with them. Calculated
disarray is marked through asymmetrical
lapels, misplaced fastenings and collars. It
is clear that as an Indian designer working
in the post-colonial context Saluja shares
common ground both conceptually and
aesthetically with Japanese designers
such as Yohji Yamamoto, Issey Miyake,
Rei Kawakubo and Junya Watanabe
known for their anti-fashion stance and
avant-garde designs. A key aspect in the

below left
Wills Lifestyle India Fashion Week,
Autumn/Winter 2014. Photograph:
Surbhi Sethi, www.headtilt.in.

below centre
Saluja constantly reinterprets traditional
dress in his collections. Here, a rich silk
sari is layered over a zippered and
cropped silk motorcycle jacket. Photograph:
Surbhi Sethi, w w w.headtilt.in.

below right
Detail of tailored *dhoti* drape trousers.
Photograph: Surbhi Sethi, www.headtilt.in.

work of Yamamoto, in particular, is his dialogue with Western traditions of men's tailoring, something for which Saluja admires him deeply. Appropriation and deconstruction of men's Western tailoring was pioneered by Japanese designers in a country where Western clothing replaced traditional forms of dress from the late 1800s onwards. Japan can be said to have a similar relationship to Western fashion as that in India, where the assimilation of Western dress codes into local culture has always been an ambiguous process. In one sense, it is a marker of progress and modernity, but it is also seen as a symbol of domination by colonial rulers, and latterly the neo-imperialism of global capitalism and the influx of Western brands into emerging economies. Deconstructing the Western suit then becomes a metaphor for deconstructing these histories and flows of power, as well as the post-colonial condition where dual identities are a daily fact of life and absorb a multiplicity of cultural flows, fashion and images into a 'work in progress' in terms of identity and authenticity.

opposite
Cord-work embroidered jacket
with silk organza shirt and jersey
jodhpur pants, 'House of Cards',
Autumn/Winter 2014.

below
Crewel-embroidered long-trailed
jacket dress, 'House of Cards',
Autumn/Winter 2014.

Pankaj & Nidhi

Pankaj & Nidhi are a husband-and-wife design partnership. They both studied at NIFT, Delhi, but met while working at the design studio of Rohit Bal.

Love struck among drapes, sequins and long hours!

Since launching their own design label in 2006, they have developed a design signature characterized by expertly constructed fusion silhouettes that play with sharp feminine tailoring, innovative cutwork, appliqué and print placement, and an aesthetic combining contemporized Indian craft techniques with global inspirations.

With 'House of Cards', Autumn/Winter 2014, for example, they were inspired when stylist Gautam Kalra suggested they watch *Blancanieves* (Snow White), a modern-day fairytale about a female Spanish bullfighter set in the 1920s. They also drew inspiration from playing cards with their iconic motifs, arcane symbolism and ornamentation. The evening wear collection they produced was composed of the Western silhouettes of long, fitted cocktail dresses and coats. Ethnic silhouettes were fused with the idea of the masculine matador into capes or sleeveless cropped full-skirted *angrakhas* paired with *jodhpurs* – an ethnic fusion

interpretation of the female tuxedo suit as an alternative to the dress for evening wear. Yet, as in their 'The Grammar of Ornament' collection, other segments of the collection showed a body-con dress with print placement that demarcated and accentuated the contours of the body. Overall the collection revealed their ability to blend influences and a cohesive, unique aesthetic that is also wearable.

The cutwork appliqué technique they used was developed from their Autumn/Winter 2012 'Wycinanki' collection which had been inspired by a trip to Poland, where they discovered the Polish folk art of cutting paper into decorative patterns. Pankaj & Nidhi translated this into an innovative technique involving cutting felt and then appliquéing it onto fine wool.

The idea evolved into more monochromatic avatars at the time we were working on 'The Grammar of Ornament'. Sometimes, a technique is born in one season and continues to evolve and develop over the next few, 'til it becomes part of our DNA.

below left
Printed jersey
dress, invitation
for 'House of Cards',
Wills Lifestyle
India Fashion
Week, Autumn/
Winter 2014.

below centre
and below right
Hand-cut appliqued
jacket dress, silk
organza shirt and
jersey pants (centre)
and hearts-and-
spades embellished
jersey and net
dress (right),
'House of Cards',
Wills Lifestyle
India Fashion
Week, Autumn/
Winter 2014.

So delicate was the rendition of this technique in the 'House of Cards' collection that many assumed it was laser cut. Instead, each piece was cut by hand, with a jacket involving as many as 500 hours of hand labour. Tiny 'biscuits' of cotton fabric were sewn by hand and layered over silk and tulle to achieve a three-dimensional effect.

The level of detail and the quality of execution places Pankaj & Nidhi in an emerging niche space in international fashion where demi-couture reflects the massive shifts taking place in luxury markets.

India has a huge market for clothes that cater to festivals and weddings. The same consumer who wears a colourful, blingy Indian outfit to a friend's Sangeet function (a song-and-dance Bollywood-style party preceding any Indian wedding ceremony) will probably be seen wearing one of our very contemporary dresses the same morning over a champagne brunch. This dichotomy is what makes India an exciting market; the contrasts are jarring and yet exciting.

It also raises questions regarding many of the issues explored in Chapters 1 and 2. How can crafts be developed into high value-added fashion and what impact will this have on the long-term future, livelihoods and opportunities for Indian artisans?

What Pankaj & Nidhi also represent is the synthesis of cultural influence and innovations of traditional Indian craft techniques that transcend categories of East and West, creating contemporary fashion that reflects the changing lifestyles of Indian consumers.

below
Printed cotton jersey
dresses, 'The Grammar
of Ornament', Autumn/
Winter 2014 (left)
and 'The Music Box',
Autumn/Winter 2013.

opposite above left
Cord-work
embroidered jacket
with silk organza
shirt and jersey
jodhpur pants,
'House of Cards',
Autumn/Winter 2014.

**opposite
above right**
Hand-cut appliqué
work on sheer net.

opposite below left
Cord-work
embroidered dress
on sheer net.

**opposite
below right**
Hand-cut appliqué
on sheer net.

right
Printed jersey
bodysuit paired with
high-necked shirt
yoke (left), printed
jersey pants and
shirt yoke (centre)
and printed jersey
dress with shirt
yoke (right), 'House
of Cards', Autumn/
Winter 2014.

of forms that extend beyond the body, based on shapes inspired by architecture and nature and expressing themes of protection, distortion and accentuation. A signature shape is a round cocoon form; of more recent work he describes this as having moved to

...many parts of the body. Sometimes the waist, knee downwards, arms or the hip. A cocoon shape comforts me. It gives my wearer an exoskeleton to protect her.

Amit Aggarwal

I never knew any dream other than being a fashion creator. Sometimes it feels it was a past life where I started my creative journey of making clothes and I am fulfilling it in this one.

Amit Aggarwal's clear sense of destiny is part of a design approach that privileges concept and fantasy. His early work displayed an uncompromising vision

He studied at NIFT, Delhi, worked and travelled extensively across Europe and Japan and then joined the Delhi-based design studio of Tarun Tahiliani whose influence can be seen in Aggarwal's deconstructive work with the sari. He then headed the design team of Creative Impex which produces for brands including Moschino, Jean Paul Gaultier and Kenzo. This led to Morphe, Aggarwal's first own design label. In 2013 he left Morphe to partner with Amit Hansraj.

What we do at the studio now is the same aesthetic but more relevant to the wearer. Hansraj added the much-needed softness of a woman's heart in my otherwise hard-shelled, architectural work.

Organic forms, fantasy and distinctive construction techniques and materials such as metal foil structure signature organic cocoon shapes. He attributes this to the duality of influences stemming from his parents.

I grew up seeing my father's industrial line drawings, his drafts for his engineering work and his relentless love for all things metal. I grew up seeing more metal being welded than flowers in a garden. I grew up to be my father's son. Metal, industrial and architectural. But the softness of the organic comes from my mother. She studied zoology and science at a time when women were not allowed to finish their studies. She couldn't pursue her career due to family conditions and

right and opposite
The front view of this dress shows a fecund silhouette, a signature of Aggarwal's work. The back of the dress shows the designer's fascination with carapaces and organic forms, Couture Collection, Spring/Summer 2015.

opposite
Detail of a bodice with corded net draped over
spandex and a sari of pleated satin-faced
georgette structured with faux metallic strips,
Sari collection, Spring/Summer 2013.

right
Kaftan in tulle structured with pliable metal
strips and an octopus clasp, Couture collection,
Autumn/Winter 2013.

right below
Dress in jersey and tulle corded with leather
and a beaded yoke, Autumn/Winter 2013.

*saw her dream through me. Today, in retrospect
what I create blends what my parents are: the
engineering of organics.*

In particular, Aggarwal is fascinated by the
interpretative ambiguity of Rorschach ink
blots as methodology for bringing ideas
into material form. He describes this as a
kind of diagnosis of the artist's inner world.

*A Rorschach opens my mind. It makes me see
the same thing differently each time. I love the
hidden forms, the symmetry and the detail. It
could be a flower, a butterfly, an alien's wings
or a human's ribs. All the things that I consider
a pleasure.*

The 'engineering of organics' is the
defining conceptual thread in Aggarwal's
work, expressed through juxtapositions:
delicate fabrics structured by 'cages'
constructed from stiff, but pliable, metal
strips. These cages take inspiration from
the carapace, the external exoskeleton
protecting the soft inner body of vertebrates
like tortoises or crustaceans such as
lobsters. The carapace was a key signature
in the work of Alexander McQueen, which
he developed notably in collections such
as 'Plato's Atlantis', Spring/Summer 2010.
It explored the morphing of humans
with amphibian creatures in a post eco-
apocalyptic world. Fashion historian Judith
Watt attributes McQueen's fascination with
organic forms built up around the body
to Japanese designer Koji Tatsuno, who

**opposite and
this page**
Couture collection,
Spring/Summer
2015.

McQueen worked for in the late 1980s.[30]
The relationship between organic forms
and the body is one of several global
conceptual currents that have concerned
designers including McQueen and his
former intern Iris Van Herpen, whose
explorations of sculptural form as fashion
push the boundaries of materials and
wearability. Aggarwal is greatly inspired
by architecture and a belief that eternal
and transcendent truths emanate from
natural forms such as air, water and fire.
These inform his attempts to capture
moments of beauty through organic forms
designed to encompass, meld and move
with the human body. It is fascinating to
consider how, if a designer such as Van
Herpen takes these conceptual influences
into rapid prototyping, this same thread
of influence plays out in Aggarwal's work
driven by the local context of the craft
skills, aesthetics and commercial
demands of the Indian market.

Exaggerated hips, a small waist,
defined shoulders and cocoon shapes
are signatures of Aggarwal's work.
As old certainties are lost the place of
women becomes a battleground for a war
between old and new values. Alienation,
dislocation and romanticism hover at the
edges of the collective unconscious and
these extenuated silhouettes paired with
the carapace denote a fierce femininity in
Aggarwal's work that seems to propose
a woman who must armour herself for
such battles. Aggarwal's 'Octopus'-
themed dresses, in particular, express
this undercurrent of social tensions.

*The idea of compression and releasing a held
form free to take the desired shape. It's like
holding something together strongly and yet
leaving it loose almost for it to enjoy its freedom!*

Since launching his couture line in 2013,
he has become far more commercial,

with exaggerated shapes toned down into figure-hugging gowns, although construction techniques and detailing retain the essence of his earlier work. This has led to wider appeal with experimental clientele who wear his creations as part of wedding celebrations or formal functions. Some of his strongest markets have proved to be abroad.

The women in the Middle East have always taken a liking to what we do, Kuwait and Riyadh are our biggest markets. They love the quirk, the special treatments we do to fabric and they love our shapes and forms. Something that highlights the shape of the body and yet somewhere distorts it.

Aggarwal's work represents a complex set of global cross-cutting flows of innovation and conceptual inspiration that go far beyond simple binaries of Western fashion or its 'Eastern' other.

opposite
Rococo earrings from
'Magniloquence'.

below
'Let your Heart Full of Gold, with
the Light Running through its
Veins Beat Louder than your
Human Heart, Full of Blood,
Hurt and Pain': 'Heart of Gold'
pendant from 'Forgotten Jewel'.

Eina Ahluwalia

Jewelry is a central part of social and
cultural life in India, marking important
life events such as marriage and childbirth.
Traditionally, married women showed their
status through bangles, *nath* (nose rings)
and *mangala sutras* (auspicious necklaces),
although increasingly these items may
also be worn as fashion statements among
the urban middle classes. Pieces such as

haath phool (ring-cum-bracelets), *payal*
(anklets), *maang tikkas* (hair jewelry)
and *nath* have also become global fashion
trends. Both men and women across
India wear jewelry based on astrological
predictions using specific gemstones
to restore character imbalances. Gold
remains a key way in which wealth is
invested. Traditional jewelry, linked to
lifecycle and gender roles, is contrasted
to fashion jewelry in the Indian market.

Ahluwalia's conceptual jewelry disrupts
this simple binary between tradition
and fashion, and she uses her designs
to comment on the social context within
which jewelry is given.

*What I like to do is redefine or recontextualize
traditional motifs and jewelry into contemporary
wearable pieces that fit our modern lifestyle
and fashion.... To me, jewelry is not about
ornamentation: it is, on the contrary, a liberating
expression of one's personality.*

Ahluwalia trained under Ruudt Peters,
a pioneering Dutch conceptual jeweller in

above
Arrowhead earrings
from 'Magniloquence'.

opposite
Durga earrings
from 'One'.

the Netherlands, and studied at Alchimia: Contemporary Jewellery School in Florence, Italy, where she now acts as India Advisor. Emmy van Leersum and Gijs Bakker are credited with starting the New Jewellery Movement in the 1970s, a pioneering approach to jewelry design that envisaged it far beyond its traditional role as marker of social status, culture and gender. For Leersum and Bakker jewelry could also be political comment or act as a vehicle to communicate profound meanings about the individuality of the wearer.

Ahluwalia works in this tradition and her jewelry makes profound connections between, and sometimes strident statements on, the relationship between power and gender in India today.

Her pieces use the traditional technique of intricate fretwork by craftsmen with whom she has worked since 2003 in her native Kolkata. These skills are being lost due to mass production, and a core ethos for Ahluwalia is to work with the craftsmen to sustain and reinterpret their work for contemporary jewelry markets. Her signature style is intricate fretwork

executed so finely that it appears to be laser or machine cut.

Although delicate in appearance, Ahluwalia's jewelry often evokes intense and profound meanings in relation to family, love, values and feminism. For example, her 2011 Lakmé Fashion Week show 'Wedding Vows' took a stand against domestic violence, which as Ahluwalia states

Permeates through social, economic, professional and religious boundaries.... The Protection of Women from Domestic Violence Act (PWDVA) was launched in India in 2005, and in a country of a over a billion people, where 45 per cent of women have suffered at least one incident of physical or psychological violence in their lifetime, every effort to spread the word about this is a drop in the ocean. Yet it needs to be done and each step has a ripple effect.

At Lakmé the first model walked onto the ramp as acoustic rock singer Josh Woodward's 'I want to Destroy Something Beautiful' played, with its hauntingly ambiguous lyrics:

These were strong motifs that invoke the power of the goddesses: swords, knives and the trishula, weapons of the goddesses themselves, all intricately worked, beautiful and grand like wedding jewels traditionally given to a bride, and yet symbols of empowerment. The underlying message is also to the families that their daughter's trousseaux must be strength, support and knowledge, and not just gold.

opposite
'Love. Respect. Protect' earrings, bangle and pendant from 'Wedding Vows', Autumn/ Winter 2011.

above
Kirpan (carved dagger) necklace from 'Wedding Vows', Autumn/ Winter 2011.

*My dear, I'll give you sixty seconds
        to disappear
And if you don't get out of here...
        who knows?
Because I've been trying to find out
        if an angel bends or breaks
Or shatters like a stone
I.... I want to destroy something beautiful
For you, I want to destroy for you.*

In a moment of catwalk high-theatre, the first model dressed in bridal red unsheathed a *kirpan* (a ceremonial dagger carried by baptized Sikhs) from the gold half-moon-shaped pendant hung from her neck. As each model followed onto the ramp the message of fighting endemic violence against women in Indian society was reiterated through jewelry that drew on religious symbols and the iconography of fierce warrior-goddesses.

My inspiration is most often life and my interaction with it. Is the life around us real, or the one we live in our heads? Perspectives – from my eyes and yours, and the space in between. The self – am I the body or the soul? The breath that defines one magical moment that I have in which to create my world.

Ahluwalia's designs neither meld into the 'normalizing fog' of Western-style fashions nor re-enact tradition as a claim to an essential 'Indian' identity. Instead, they draw on Dutch approaches to conceptual jewelry and traditional Indian motifs, forging pieces that critique structures of power and gendered inequality within Indian society itself.

Generation next

opposite
Sneha Arora, 'Leak',
Spring/Summer 2014.

Urban metros Delhi, Mumbai, Pune and Bangalore are now fashion destinations. Management companies staging lavish corporate-sponsored events, media avidly covering designers' shows and consumers who buy and style their designs all demarcate these cities as part of fashion's new global geography. Outside such urban metros, small cities and towns are now key destinations for luxury brands to mass-retail ethnic wear. However, challenges remain, including scaling-up business, standardization, lack of retail infrastructure and how to support early career development for young design talent. These challenges are documented in seminal studies of the industry by Hindol Sengupta[31] and Shefalee Vasudev.[32]

The average spend on day versus occasion wear is increasing among affluent middle-class consumers. India's youth, fetishized by marketing professionals as the country's 'democratic dividend', are an important target market: an estimated 50 per cent of the population is under the age of 25. Recent retail market developments include e-commerce attracting private equity fund investment, as well as expansion of international fast-fashion brands in India's metros. While some view this adversely, others sense opportunity, as large retailers help boost consumer appetite for fashion. Saket Dhankar runs Lakmé Fashion Week for the title sponsor, and is head of the fashion vertical for IMG Reliance.

Bridal wear is not the only option for Indian designers to scale up. Brands like Anita Dongre's diffusion lines 'AND' and 'Global Desi' are among the most successful examples of Indian designers scaling up through the high street market. A good understanding of the urban Indian middle-class consumer, who wants to be trendy yet price conscious, is where there is huge potential for designers to expand. Indian designers have great strength in the 'Indo-Fusion' or 'Contemporary ethnic-wear' categories which are extremely popular with Indian consumers, and this is where the fast-fashion brands have no offerings at all. While the established designers are still fighting it out in the bridal space, the younger designers are exploring unchartered territories like the western prêt-à-porter space. They also want to make a mark in the international market.

right
Pernia Qureshi, emerald
high-waisted skirt with
embellished blouse.

far right
Nikhil Thampi, long-
sleeved blouse and
lehenga embroidered
with *kathakali*-
inspired motif,
Autumn/Winter 2013.

The diverse range of designers in this chapter demonstrates how Indian fashion continues to provide exciting adaptations to a dynamic, challenging, and in many ways unchartered market. Both silhouettes and aesthetic surfaces represent a variety of responses to this market context. They create ethnic garments in monochromatic hues or decorated with motifs borrowed from Indian culture, cognisant of these as part of a globally circulating set of images and fantasies of India. There is also the reinvention of Indian culture and aesthetics into a global frame. Nikhil Thampi, for example, recasts South Indian dance alongside British punk. Conversely, Josh Goraya produces Western silhouettes with surfaces that resist being geographically associated with preconceived notions of Indian aesthetics. Although their aesthetic strategies are vastly different they both embody what anthropologist Arjun Appadurai calls deterritorialization.[33] For Appadurai, we now live in globally imagined worlds, not simply local communities. This is evident where hip, cosmopolitan re-readings of local culture are recast within a globalized framework, and global styles of fashion are absorbed into Indian designers aesthetics and practice. Unlike in other non-Western contexts where local dress has been superseded by Western dress, India has a long history of sartorial fusion creating a continuous mixing of styles into the unique phenomenon known as 'Desi-chic'.[34] Yogesh Chaudhary explains that his approach to design reinvigorates ethnic silhouettes with reference to Western fashion trends such as crop-tops and bomber jackets, observing how women around him and on the streets are dressing. In this he tunes into this ability to 'mix' styles so that Indian fashion is always more than just a sum of its parts. If we follow Barthes' theory that clothing is akin to language, then a good way to think about the design language here is 'fluency'.[35] These young designers fluidly negotiate complex dynamics between tradition and modernity; local rootedness and global cosmopolitanism, providing a new language of how to articulate being Indian in a globalizing world in the process.

above
Pernia Qureshi.

right
Josh Goraya, Spring/
Summer 2014.

An e-commerce site allows a much larger customer base than a physical store. My client is any and every woman from around the world of all age groups. This site is especially convenient for those in tier 2 and 3 cities, who do not need to travel to a big metro to get their hands on designer clothing. It is also a very convenient site for non-resident Indians since they are familiar with these designers.

Pernia Qureshi and Pernia's Pop-up Shop

In addition, Qureshi has launched her own label, a reflection of her personal style with distinctive collections of contemporized ethnic silhouettes.

I find the whole process of conceptualizing a collection, designing and having the collection made into actual pieces, very exciting and riveting. [Of her e-commerce venture she adds] *The most important thing is our curation. I am personally involved in every decision, when it comes to curation, and we are very particular about the kind of designers and clothes we want featured on the website.*

In Chapter 1 we saw how the Tahilianis broke the mould by launching India's first multi-designer boutique in Mumbai; 25 years later in 2012, Pernia Qureshi provided another milestone in Indian fashion, launching Pernia's Pop-up Shop, a curated multi-designer e-commerce experience.

right
Lace maxi dress by Urvashi Kaur featured in editorial imagery for Pernia's Pop-up Shop online magazine.

opposite
Black maxi dress with floral bodice designed by Pernia Qureshi.

All designed by
Pernia Qureshi.

Launching with just 17 designers, Pernia's Pop-up Shop now includes over 200 designer names.

The purpose of starting this website was to bring the plethora of talented Indian designers together and give them access to a global platform to showcase their designs. Also, many young designers are experimenting with styles, trying to create their own niche. I want to support that, so we have a wide array of designs ranging from ethnic to contemporary and fusion wear.

The online store is distinctive for its highly produced content including an in-house e-magazine featuring celebrity videos, contests and styling advice.

In the past few years, I feel people have become more aware and responsive to fashion. People don't buy clothes just because it is from an established designer anymore. They want to buy something that excites them or that works with their personal style, they want something 'new'.

above
Printed dress by Turquoise and Gold,
editorial imagery from 'The Travel Issue'
of Pernia's Pop-up Shop online magazine.

right
Yami Gautam in a rose-gold sequin sheer
dress by Sailex for Pernia's Pop-up Shop.

*I find the whole process of conceptualizing
a collection, designing and having the
collection made into actual pieces, very
exciting and riveting.*

opposite
Actress Kalki Koechlin in a cropped
bomber jacket from 'The Two Teeshirts',
Summer/Resort 2014. Stylist: Aastha
Sharma; photograph: Vishesh Verma
for Maxim India, March 2014.

Yogesh Chaudhary

right
'Miss Pac-in District',
Autumn/ Winter
2012. Photograph:
Ishaan Nair.

Young Haryana-born designer Yogesh
Chaudhary studied at NIFT, Delhi, and
then for an MA at NID. In 2010 he won the
Van Heusen Emerging Designer of the
Year award and then showed as part of the
GenNext platform at Lakmé Fashion Week,
Spring/Summer 2012. His label 'Surendri'
is named after his mother. His view of
the dynamic between India and Western
fashion is unequivocal.

*Personally, I would like to blur the outline
between Indian/ethnic and Western wear.
For me, all of it comes under one category:
ready-to-wear. I observe what people around
me are wearing. It helps me understand what
they might want to wear next.*

Each year Chaudhary's collections reveal
the way in which he interprets the dynamic
between Indian and Western fashion with
print playing a central role. For Autumn/
Winter 2012 his 'Miss Pac' sari printed with
iconic Pac-Man motifs was based on his
childhood obsession with the video game.

Many permutations of ethnic wear
exist, given labels such as fusion, Indo-
Western, or ethnic-chic. These attempt to
capture the dynamic where Indian and
Western silhouettes and surface decoration
meet. As new generations of designers
absorb an ever-multiplying global flow
of images, styles, concepts and designs
for a transforming fashion market, so the
dialogue between Indian and Western
dress forms develops its own continuity
of referencing. Evident in Chaudhary's
work is the distillation of already-adapted
silhouettes to new expressions, further
reinforcing Indian fashion's own logic
outside of *a priori* definitions of fashion
as an inherently 'Western' phenomenon.
For example, the *salwar kameez* (a loose
tunic and pants) was traditionally the
dress of North Indian Muslims, Punjabis,
Hindus and Sikhs as discussed by Clare
Wilkinson-Weber.[36] In the 1960s and 1970s
it became associated with a specific film
character type, the college girl, a middle-
class, university-educated heroine. This led,
as illustrated by Rachel Dwyer and Divia
Patel, to its adoption by the middle classes
across India in place of the sari.[37] In films
such as *Chandni* (1989) and *Dil Chahta Hai*
(2001) stylistic innovations turned the *salwar*

'Personally I would like to blur the line between Indian/ ethnic and western wear. For me all of it comes under one category which is ready-to-wear.'

left
Cropped hooded bomber jacket
and skirt from 'The Two Teeshirts',
Summer/Resort 2014. Photograph
courtesy of Pernia's Pop-up Shop.

above
'The Two Teeshirts', Summer/Resort 2014.
Photographed for the e-commerce site
of Pernia's Pop-up Shop. Photograph:
courtesy of Pernia's Pop-up Shop.

kameez into fashionable ethnic chic. For Summer/Resort 2014 Chaudhary spliced the *kameez* tunic into a cropped bomber jacket and skirt over *salwar* pants, matching it to the *dupatta* in a sporty print. He focuses on capturing the dynamic spirit of how young women are dressing, combining ethnic and Western shapes and prints, as seen in Indian towns and cities.

The 'Surendri' woman is young, quirky and confident and carries herself with infallible ease. She is a global citizen and understands fashion, its impact and influence. With the plethora of opportunities available in India and the kind of market size, the major challenge is more about trying to cater to it in its entirety more than anything else.

While designers in Europe face the challenge of integrating a conceptual theme across a collection that may include evening wear, separates and outerwear, Indian designers face the additional challenge of incorporating their overall concept into a further division between ethnic and Western silhouettes that guarantee wider market reach. An especially strong signature of Chaudhary's work is how he meets this challenge, while rendering a conceptual theme across a collection of ethnic and western silhouettes. 'Dip Dip Dip My Sunken Ship', Summer/Resort 2013, was a good example of this, also exemplifying his fresh and playful approach to self-expression through fashion.

opposite and right
'Dip Dip Dip My
Sunken Ship',
Summer/Resort 2013.
Photograph:
Ishaan Nair.

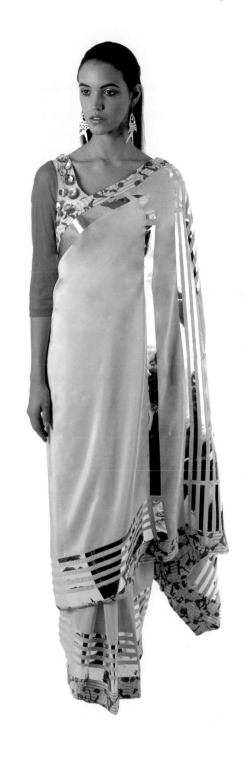

Ruchika Sachdeva

right and opposite
Bodice, Spring/
Summer 2015.

Delhi-based designer Ruchika Sachdeva's signature style is minimal and clean, something she attributes to her interest in menswear (despite the fact she studied womenswear for a BA at the London College of Fashion). Fit and function as opposed to ornamentation define her work. She called her label 'Bodice' because

Bodice is the basic and most fundamental block used in pattern making – the science of making

2D paper patterns used to cut fabric before sewing them together as final garments. Since pattern making was my strength, I thought of naming my brand after what I was most fascinated by: the bodice block.

She started 'Bodice' after realizing that there was an absence of premium everyday clothing in a designer market dominated by expensive occasion wear. Her designs are characterized by loose-fitting linear silhouettes that allow for freedom of movement while emphasizing the shoulders – so retaining the structured style of menswear. Inspired by androgyny and Western traditions of men's tailoring, Sachdeva also works with traditional ethnic silhouettes such as the *kurta*. This results in an aesthetic that transcends categorization as either ethnic dress or Western minimalism but proposes an internationalist interpretation of functional yet aesthetically appealing clothing.

Fresh from design college she interned for Vivienne Westwood, renowned for her championing of environmental and social causes in fashion. Sachdeva is quietly taking that influence forward. After the

opposite
Autumn/Winter 2014.

above left and right
Looks from Bodice
Spring/Summer 2015
display the influence
of men's tailoring
and embody
Sachdeva's vision
of creating
a premium
contemporary
day-to-evening
wear brand for
the Indian market.

horrors of the Rana Plaza disaster in
2013 a new venture Indelust launched
its online portal for the best in Indian
design grounded in principles of social
responsibility along the supply chain,
with Sachdeva as one of its hand-picked
designers. Sachdeva also features as
part of Priya Kishore's curation of Indian
designers in the online portal for Bombay
Electric. Along with Pernia's Pop-up Shop
these sites are part of the emerging field
of e-commerce, allowing unprecedented
access to India's brightest young design
talent. In 2014 Sachdeva's success was
consolidated when she won the annual
Indian edition of the Vogue Fashion Fund.

*We have pioneered a polished aesthetic that
continues to play with ideas of modernity and
exploration while working with indigenous
materials and techniques. This formula has
produced a recognizable identity, which is
carefully constructed through integration of
androgyny and the reinvention of classics with
a subtle hint of irony. While treading the line
between experimental, modern, Indian design
and comfortable confident ensembles, we search
for the intriguing yet enduring balance.*

opposite
Spring/Summer 2014.

right
From 'the shirt.i.just.made', 2012.
Model: Zelig Joyce Wilson;
photograph: Cho Hang Siu Rex.

were the men's suits where pinstripes, associated with the traditional business suit, graduated into razors, creating the illusion of stripes drawn by downstrokes of the blades. This playfully suggested the idea of masculinity being remade on a daily basis through social acts of shaving and dressing.

I referenced the contradiction between vanity and the natural human body. How we try to go against the rules of nature and manipulate it, both men and women, and its part as an androgynous strong dynamic between them. As a metaphor, I exploited the image of a shaving razor to illustrate this metamorphosis. Our label has always used this motif, an 'old-school shaving

Josh Goraya

Born in Rajasthan, Josh Goraya graduated from NIFT, Delhi in 2006 with an award for creative excellence. He then spent five years working for Rohit Gandhi and Rahul Khanna and launched his eponymous label in 2011. In 2013 he won 'Let's Design', supported by Cotton Council International (CCI) and the FDCI.

Goraya's design signature rests on a bedrock of masculine tailoring, luxe sportswear, a unique print aesthetic and detailing.

We try to give a fresh and more modern look to a traditional silhouette such as bandhgala *by adding that one interesting element or a twist like an unusual base fabric or buttons to make it more contemporary and eclectic. Or we manipulate the pattern and shift the seams and darts to make it more experimental. Also, the length and fit is something we love to play with. Indian men's fashion is now not only about red carpets and high profile gatherings, the identity of men's fashion is influenced by what you see on the streets every day.*

'Alter Nature', his Spring/Summer 2014 collection featured a traditional men's shaving razor as its key motif, reworked in different prints across men's suits and shirts and women's sports-influenced dresses and pants. Especially striking

left
Masculine tailoring
and sportswear
form the bedrock of
Goraya's approach
to both menswear
and womenswear,
Autumn/Winter 2014.

right
Autumn/Winter 2014.

below left
Portrait of Josh
Goraya with tattoos
of his signature
old-school shaving-
razor design.

below right
Autumn/Winter 2014.

opposite
Men's tailoring
codes are spliced
and subverted by
Goraya.

overleaf above
The shaving razor interpreted
in different prints for menswear,
Spring/Summer 2014.

overleaf below
Sportswear-influenced looks for
womenswear, Spring/Summer
2014.

*razor'. We chose the razor as it represents
the pursuit of vanity and since we do a lot of
androgynous clothing, we feel it connects both
the sexes as it's used by both and hair can send
such powerful gendered messages. The razor
alters nature to make it look more beautiful
according to social conventions of grooming or
completely removing body/facial hair.*

Goraya focuses on Western silhouettes and
chooses neither to mix them with ethnic
silhouettes nor to infuse them with surface
aesthetics that in any way reference Indian
culture or aesthetics or ideas of these.

*I feel fortunate to have amazing Indian textiles,
embroideries and colours at my disposal, but
the label Josh Goraya is certainly not trying
to sell India to the world. Even though the
major emphasis is given to Indian textiles and
hand-woven fabrics, our designs still don't have
any geographical representation or any ethnic
inclination whatsoever; the pieces are such that
they could be worn easily by any individual in any
corner of this world without standing out on
the basis of culture or ethnicity.*

which he had no formal training: he felt apprehensive about how his designs would be received and wondered if he could face the pressures of a design career. His second collection was called 'Survival'. He describes it as

Depicting strength, fierceness, free-spiritedness, survival, pushing forward and growing. This in so many ways was like my journey as a designer.

Nikhil Thampi

below
Dramatic contrast between linear tailoring and fluid drapes, Summer/Resort 2013.

opposite
Kathakali-inspired print, Lakmé Fashion Week, Mumbai, Autumn/Winter 2013.

Part of Qureshi's goal with Pernia's Pop-up Shop is to provide a platform for emerging designers, providing them with fast-track access to essential back-end supply operations and consumer markets. One such emerging designer supported by Qureshi is Nikhil Thampi. Thampi only launched his designer label in 2011, yet his success has been rapid, gaining him popularity among young celebrities, leading to all-important media coverage. His first collection was called 'Mixed Emotions', a reflection of his state of mind on launching into a career for

'Untamed', Summer/Resort 2014, made use of rose-gold metal flowers, providing a feminine accent to bold, boxy jackets paired with fluid pants, a look photographed almost countless times on celebrities.

South Indian by birth, Thampi has also injected a relatively rare flavour of south Indian aesthetics into ethnic formal wear, which, as shown in Chapter 1, is often dominated by the heritage of North Indian royal history. For Lakmé Autumn/Winter 2013 he drew inspiration from *kathakali*, a dance form originating in the southernmost Indian state of Kerala. Traditional Indian garments including saris, *lehengas* and *anarkalis* were given an edge through cut-out panels in a cohesive palette of black, white and gold. The print motif was the face of a *kathakali* dancer. Thampi framed this local inspiration in terms of British

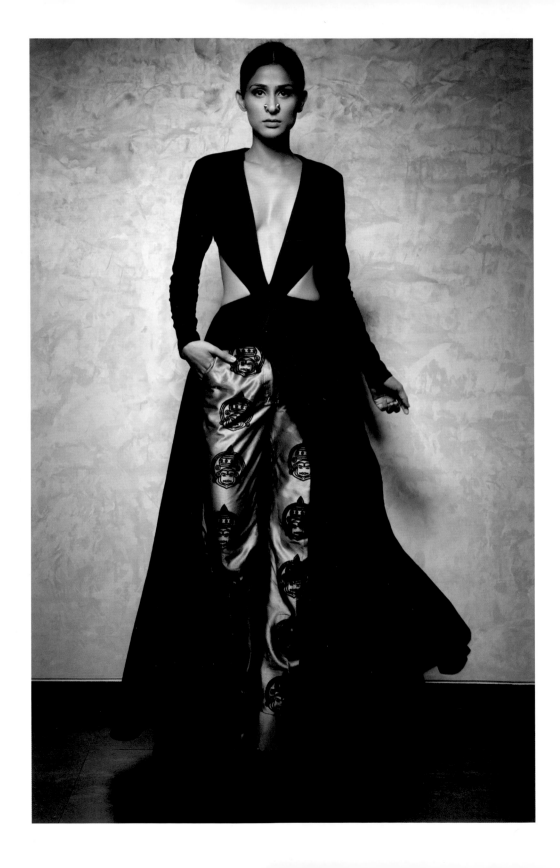

opposite
A black linen cut-out *anarkali* with
a deep centre split at the front and
gold trousers with a *kathakali*-
inspired print, Autumn/Winter 2013.

below
Autumn/Winter 2013.

opposite
Lakmé Fashion
Week, Mumbai,
Autumn/Winter 2013.

below
Rose-gold metal
flowers accent
fluid drapes and
cropped jackets,
'Unframed', Spring/
Summer 2014.

punk, making intriguing links between *kathakali* and punk's sub-cultural style and anti-conformist stance.

Kathakali is associated with fluid movements, loud colours and over-the-top facial expressions. There is a fierce fearlessness exuded from these dancers when they perform. I wanted to accentuate that emotion but not in a conventional manner and that's when I thought of interspersing punk elements.

His designs for women play with the dynamic between sharp masculine tailoring and signature flesh-revealing cut-outs and fluid drapes. He runs the gamut of silhouettes from Western through ethnic wear, creating jumpsuits, shift dresses, saris, gowns, swimwear, tailored jackets and pants, but lends them common ground through a balance between structure and pared-back fluidity.

I like the sharp contrast that is reflected with the use of cotton blends (generally used in menswear) along with materials like crêpe, organza and various other diaphanous fabrics. My main goal is to ensure that unique designs, which highlight women's beauty, make them feel sexy and confident in their skin, and are the perfect balance of comfort and style. I've always said 'It's not about feeling the fabric, it's about fabricating one's feelings' and that is my constant endeavour through my creations.

My liking for prints developed when I was working for a domestic retail brand after college. I was given the t-shirt category of the brand, which in the beginning I hated!...but somewhere down the line I grew to like print. It has kind of become my USP.

Sharp tailoring is combined with unusual detailing such as linear keyholes and sinuous cuts on jacket lapels.

I love tailored and structured clothing and there is so much to learn in the techniques that every time I make a collection I learn new ways to construct. I have this infinite love for details. I feel the details recite the story of the garment. The more detailed it is, the more you are intrigued.

Sneha Arora

below
'I Believe I Can Fly', Spring/Summer 2013.

opposite
'Leak', Spring/Summer 2014.

Sneha Arora grew up in Bengal and studied design at NIFT, Kolkata. She has participated in the 'Future of Fashion' and 'Who's Next' Autumn/Winter 2014 and Spring/Summer 2015 programmes curated by new talent showcase Not Just a Label. Her designs represent a relaxed, feminine approach to masculine tailoring for women, with distinctive use of print placement and unusual tailored details. Like many young fashion students, she worked for an export house after graduating.

Arora's signature of playing with the dynamic between masculine tailoring and feminine shapes is a response to the ambiguities of changing gender roles, where many women now run their own business or occupy high-level managerial positions in the corporate world.

My clients are very diverse in age: I have 25-year-old clients and clients who are 50 as

*I wanted to develop a line
which makes the woman who
wears it strong and confident.*

*well...they are strong women who want to look
different and powerful. To an extent, strength
and men are correlated in our society, so if you
want to be strong you have to be masculine.
I wanted to develop a line which makes the
woman who wears it strong and confident.*

Her collections are conceptualized around
a central theme, for example 'Leak', Spring/
Summer 2014 featured print placements:
florets of colour blooming organically.

*The inspiration comes from my own experience
of trying to make everything so perfect that you
miss out on enjoying the process of creation.
It's about allowing yourself to be human,
about making mistakes, falling and getting lost.
Enjoy the imperfections of life and allow yourself
to 'leak' – because broken pieces sometimes
make better art and perfect lives don't make
as interesting a story.*

Her clothing has an identity that cannot
be pinned down to any particular
geographical area and this is part of
her goal to expand internationally.

*The international market is very important. I'm
working very hard on getting into it. We all want
to be global, don't we?!*

opposite and right
'Leak', Spring/
Summer 2014.

opposite
'Shakuntala', Autumn/Winter
2014. The jewelry embodies the
legend of Shakuntala who lived
in harmony with the flora and
fauna of the forests in the foothills
of the Himalayas.

Milan-based Creative Academy run by
Swiss luxury conglomerate Richemont
(she also interned for Montblanc, part of
Richemont's portfolio).

Her jewelry collections mix inspiration
from both traditional culture and global
design influences. For example, her 2014
debut collection 'Please Have a Seat' was
inspired after visiting the Louvre Museum
in Paris, while she was studying in Europe.

Mrinalini Chandra

*There was a deeper connotation to the theme,
'Please Have a Seat'. It was about trying to
remind people to start living small joys,
to relax and enjoy the moment!*

below
Unexpected twists
on traditional
jewelry defined
'Please Have a Seat',
Summer/Resort 2014.

Closely aligned to the growth of clothing
design has been the emergence of
accessories and jewelry. Lakmé Fashion
Week now regularly showcases accessory
designers and Mumbai-based Mrinalini
Chandra is one of its protégées. She
studied accessory design at NIFT, Delhi,
and was awarded a scholarship to study
for an MA in luxury jewelry design at the

The perhaps unexpected inspiration
of chairs was translated into bracelets,
drop earrings, cuffs and a memorable
Lakmé Fashion Week finale, where model
Kanishtha Dhankar walked slowly down
the ramp with her arms hung with *kalire*.
Kalire are traditionally associated with
Sikh weddings in the Punjab and are
formed by elaborate umbrella-shaped
ornaments strung from the bride's bangles.
In Chandra's *kalire* the ornaments were
replaced by dainty circles of chairs set
around miniature tables hung from the
arms in graceful kinesis.

*Kalire are unique to Sikh weddings in the
Punjab, and are delicate in nature and jingle
with movement. There is huge sentimental
value associated with them because on her
wedding day the bride puts on red and white
chooda (bangles) to signify her status as a bride
and to express their good wishes the bride's
relatives tie the kalire onto these bangles. Later
in the day she has to jingle the kalire over the
heads of the young unmarried women in the
family. It is believed that by doing this, they will
be the next to get married.*

Her second collection, called 'Shakuntala',
was inspired by the fifth-century AD
classical poet Kalidasa and his
interpretations of stories from *The
Mahabharata*. Kalidasa tells the story of

opposite
'Please Have a Seat',
Lakmé Fashion
Week, Mumbai,
Summer/Resort 2014.
Model Kanishtha
Dhankar walks with
long *kalire* attached
to bangles.

right
'Please Have a Seat',
Summer/Resort
2014 explored the
symbolism of the
humble chair,
translating it into
unexpected twists
on traditional
Indian jewelry.

below and opposite
'Shakuntala',
Lakmé Fashion Week,
Mumbai, Autumn/
Winter 2014.

Shakuntala, the child of a female heavenly spirit and a mortal man, who is raised by a *rishi* in an enchanted jungle in the foothills of the Himalayas. In the forest she has to wait for Dushyanta, her abiding love, and takes comfort from the forest around her. Chandra interprets Shakuntala's mythical affinity with the flora and fauna of the forest as a form of wild spiritualism, translating this into the ornamented forms of the jewelry collection. Flowers, leaves, insects, monkeys, fish and singing birds populate necklaces, earrings, cuffs and collars.

My idea of jewelry is very ornate, dynamic and fun. I like to play with forms: the play of movement and intricate mechanisms. I create little installations to be worn as body adornments. The thing that I like best about jewelry is its relationship with the wearer. The way it settles on the body is what makes it unique. For instance, the swaying of earrings by the ear makes it prettier, the jingling of bangles on the wrist is so fascinating. Here, in India, every piece of jewelry has a significance to the part of body on which it is being worn.

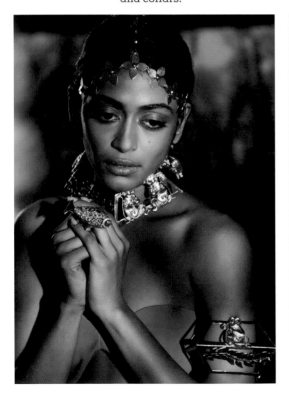

opposite
Spring/Summer 2014.

right
Shahani's diffusion up-cycling line
'Heart to Haat' ('haat' means market
in Hindi).

Karishma Shahani

Many young designers do not want their designs to look obviously 'Indian', wary of overriding preconceptions of Indian fashion as colourful kitsch and glitz. In contrast, Karishma Shahani faces the challenge of preconceptions head on. Her collections distill what she calls 'colours picked from traditional paintings of Indian gods', creating wearable clothing built up in layers with pieces that draw on local styles of dressing. In 2010, she graduated with a BA Hons in womenswear design from the London College of Fashion, winning the best surface textiles award for her year. While there she was influenced by the growing movement of ethical and sustainable fashion embodied in the college's Centre for Sustainable Fashion (CSF). Thus a core focus of her work centres on concepts of up-cycling, sustainable processes of making and the ethics of production.

I felt my time away from India made me more aware of the diversity the country had to offer and drew me closer to it. It gave me the desire to travel and explore and learn about things I had for so long before taken for granted. My graduation collection was an ode to where I belonged and all its inspirations that stemmed very strongly from my education in a country so different from where I belonged. It was

purely this balancing acting of my roots and my education that resulted in 'Yatra' and its details.

'Yatra', 2011, featured loose shapes in bright vegetable-dyed hues with vivid bursts of embroidery that nodded to craft tradition while rendering it in ways that encouraged a fresh perspective. Delicate webs of sequins and beading accentuate Shahani's work but remain subdued rather than overbearing texture and balance. Her signature is to reinterpret forms of embroidery and techniques such as tie-dye that have become such formulaic cliches in the global trend known as boho-chic. 'Khoj', Autumn/Winter 2014, is a good example of how she gave tie-dye a fresh take through neat, graphic lines.

Shahani's diffusion line cleverly called 'Heart to Haat' (*haat* means weekly market and has become associated with up-scale craft sellers in urban India) plays on the link between craft and the

opposite
'Yatra: The Land of Dreams',
Shahani's graduate collection at
the London College of Fashion,
Spring/Summer 2011.

left and below
Shahani's fresh interpretation
of traditional clamp-dyeing,
Autumn/Winter 2014.
Photographs: Vaishnav Praveen.

ethos of sustainable livelihoods, as well
as the global trend towards craft-based
production as a form of distinctive,
individual dressing in response to mass
production and fast fashion. All of the
pieces for this collection are made from
up-cycled textiles.

Conclusion

This book has provided an overview of Indian fashion designers, contextualizing their work in social, cultural and economic aspects of contemporary India. Inevitably, given the inherently fast pace of fashion, in several years time, some of this analysis may need updating. However, what this book aims to provide, with a view to future continuity, is a conceptual framework with which we may understand and navigate the diverse aesthetics of Indian fashion.

Several themes run throughout, which aim not to be a definitive reckoning of Indian fashion, but to provoke further debate. They implicitly raise a series of classic theoretical questions: what is fashion? Who and what is it for, why does it change and what does this say about gender, culture and society? Although this is a book about the vision of India's designers, they themselves work in creative response to the demands of a consumer market with a middle class the size of the population of Australia, where '… *keeping up with the Kapoors, the Joneses and the Kardashians*' determines the role of fashion in the struggle for class status and acceptance into both local and global frames of identity and belonging.[38]

A related thread is the cultural importance of cloth in Indian society, highlighted through the continued reverence of Gandhian philosophy in designers' work with handloom and the role of cloth in forging a shared material and visual language of identity. As part of a *New Swadeshi* movement handloom and craft have become strategies of distinction, that express particular values surrounding consumption's relationship to identity as well as a nationalist view of luxury as part of India's post-colonial resurgence.[39] Consider the dress designed by Rahul Mishra on the cover of this book. It is hand-embroidered with delicate representations of flora and fauna, evoking Mughal-era miniature paintings. At the centre sits a peacock, subtly referencing the Indian national bird, a symbol of grace, beauty and joy, which morphs into tessellated hexagons, representing the interconnectedness of the urban and rural, human activity and environmental impact. This visual metaphor for India itself, and the challenges facing its development, is woven and embroidered into the very fabric of the dress. There can be no stronger riposte to the prejudice that dismisses fashion as mere 'frivolous surface' than the aesthetics, highly skilled craft techniques and ethos behind Mishra's designs. Suzy Menkes writes about the unique contribution to international fashion made by designers like Mishra who are working in this vein.[40] This confluence of aesthetics and ethics runs like a thread though many of the visions of designers working with handloom and traditional craft techniques.

Another common theme is the sari, understood through its historical role in symbolizing national identity and particularly the all-Indian mother, making its role in contemporary fashion powerful, yet sometimes controversial, situated as it is in the politics of non-Western dress. That it finds such diverse expression, from the purist unstitched drapes of Sanjay Garg to the cultural (crucially not literal!) 'weightiness' of a Sabyasachi sari, or the innovative design language of Abraham & Thakore's work with regional weaving styles, is testimony to the sari's continuing role in defining the contours of the body politic. The sari as a garment confers both elegance and a sense of national identity to the wearer. But the sari drape also articulates a global continuity of design language from, for example, the *flou* techniques of Paris couture or the influence of Madame Vionnet's work with draping and cutting on the bias of Japanese designers such as Yohji Yamamoto. These global concepts of the drape articulate the design language of the sari drape in terms of international fashion, reinforcing the modernity of uniquely local practices such as the deconstructed sari drapes of Gaurav Gupta or Arjun Saluja.

A review of many of the silhouettes across the chapters shows how reinvention, deconstruction and splicing of ethnic and Western traditions expresses the common concern among designers of 'making sense of being Indian'. From Khanna's half-drape saris, Mishra's biker-*anarkalis*, Shivan & Narresh's bikini-sari, or Chaudhary's crop-top version of the *salwar kameez*.

All this connects the sphere of fashion to the sphere of art, not only in the specific cases of the designers explored in Chapter 4, but also in the far broader sense of how both fashion and art sit, as aspects of public visual culture, at the forefront of making sense of Indian identity in the post-colonial era. This has been thought of as a paradox: how to be Indian, yet also modern, when modernity has been so closely linked to the West, its culture and mores as part of a problematic history of colonialism and latterly a 'Euro-American-centred present'.[41] The fact that despite the long history of assimilation of Western dress into Indian wardrobes, in everyday practice it is not called 'global' or cosmopolitan dress, but is still popularly called Western wear by individuals and on signage in Indian department stores, attests to the importance of these different styles of clothing in making sense of what it means to be Indian today. We can see, then, that Indian designers have necessarily embraced a diverse range of propositions for dressing that are intimately tied up in notions of beauty, the body and cultural identity. The contemporary Indian fashion industry emerged as part of the social, cultural and economic context of the post-colonial era. Its aesthetic surfaces and approaches to design cross boundaries of time and space, incorporating ancient techniques into cross-cultural flows of imagery, blending ideas of tradition and modernity and forging a design language as rich, diverse and ever-unfolding as India itself.

Endnotes

1 Brosius, C., 2010. *India's Middle Class: Urban Forms of Leisure, Consumption and Prosperity*. London: Routledge.

2 Breward, C., 2012. *Fashion: The Oxford Handbook of The History of Consumption*. Oxford: Oxford University Press; Klaffke, P., 2003. *Spree: A Cultural History of Shopping*. Vancouver: Arsenal Pulp Press.

3 Thomas, D., 2007. *Deluxe: How Luxury Lost its Lustre*. New York: Penguin Books.

4 Editor's blog. 16 May 2011. 'Abu-Sandeep Style Directors for GVK Wedding in Hyderabad.' *Wedding Sutra*. http://weddingsutra.com/blog/index.php/2011/05/16/abu-jani-and-sandeep-khosla-style-directors-for-the-gvk-wedding/

5 Brosius, C., 2010, *ibid.*, p. 73.

6 Payal and Priyanka, 31 December 2013, 'Rewind 2013'. High Heel Confidential: www.highheelconfidential.com/fashion-round/

7 Sandhu, A., 2014. *Indian Fashion: Tradition, Innovation, Style*. London: Bloomsbury, p. 102.

8 Brosius, C., 2010, *ibid.*, p. 304.

9 'Anita Dongre's Tech-Savvy Jaipur Bride (Exclusive)'. *Vogue India*, 21 August 2013. https://www.youtube.com/watch?v=CYBqSAdzmU0

10 Brosius, C., 2010, *ibid.*, pp. 304–306.

11 Jay, P., 2013. *Fashionably Gandhian: Craft, Contemporary Fashion Design and Luxury in Pursuit of 'the Cloth of Freedom'*. PhD thesis; University College London.

12 Jay, P., 2016. *Indian Khadi Cloth: From National Fabric to Luxury Fashion*. London: Bloomsbury Academic.

13 Patel, D., 2014. *India: Contemporary Design: Fashion, Graphics, Interiors*. Delhi: Roli Books.

14 Khaire, M., 2011. 'Context, Agency, and Identity: The Indian Fashion Industry and Traditional Indian Crafts.' *Business History Review*, 85 (2).

15 Pinney, C., 1999. 'On Living in the Kal(i) yug: Notes from Nagda, Madhya Pradesh.' *Contributions to Indian Sociology* (1–2): 77–106.

16 Mazzarella, W., 2003. *Shoveling Smoke: Advertising and Globalization in Contemporary India*. Durham, N.C. and London: Duke University Press.

17 Chapman, J., 2005. *Emotionally Durable Design: Objects, Experiences and Empathy*. London: Earthscan.

18 Niessen, S., 2003. 'Fashion-Nation: A Japanese Globalization Experience and a Hong Kong Dilemma' in Niessen, S., Leshkowich, A. M., and C. Jones (eds), 2003. *Re-orienting Fashion: the Globalization of Asian Dress*. Oxford: Berg.

19 Crill, R., 1999. *Indian Embroidery*. London: Victoria and Albert Museum.

20 Karlekar, M., 2005. *Re-visioning the Past: Early Photography in Bengal 1875–1915*. Delhi and Oxford: Oxford University Press.

21 Ramaswamy, S., 2009. *The Goddess and the Nation: Mapping Mother India*. Durham N.C.: Duke University Press.

22 Kapur, G., 2000. *When was Modernism: Essays on Contemporary Cultural Practice in India*. Delhi: Tulika Books, p. 167.

23 Sandhu, A., 2014. *ibid.*, p. 15.

24 Vasudev, S., 12 July 2014. 'Gaurav Gupta: Strictly Ballroom', LiveMint. http://www.livemint.com/Leisure/t50LKY4kbzzQDhbN0VyaZK/Gaurav-Gupta--Strictly-ballroom.html

25 Arnold, R., 2009. *Fashion: A Very Short Introduction*. Oxford: Oxford University Press.

26 Jumabhoy, Z., 2010. 'Introduction', in *The Empire Strikes Back: Indian Art Today*. London: Jonathan Cape, p. 56.

27 Ramaswamy, S., 2009, *ibid*.

28 Sinha, C., 22 October 2012. 'Kallol Datta's inspiration.' Crossing Over – Fragments from a Journey.

http://chinkisinha.blogspot.co.uk/2012/10/kallol-dattas-inspiration.html

29 Geczy, A., 2013. *Fashion and Orientalism: Dress, Textiles and Culture from the 17th to the 21st Century*. London: Bloomsbury, p. 182.

30 Watt, J., 2013. *Alexander McQueen: The Life and Legacy*. New York: HarperCollins.

31 Sengupta, H., 2009. *Ramp Up: The Business of Indian Fashion*. Delhi: Pearson.

32 Vasudev, S., 16 October 2010. 'Free-to-Wear-Anything Country.' *The Indian Express*. http://archive.indianexpress.com/news/freetowearanything-country/698459/

33 Appadurai, A., 1996. *Modernity at Large: Cultural Dimensions in Globalization*. Minnesota: Minnesota Press.

34 Sandhu, A., 2014. *Indian Fashion: Tradition, Innovation, Style*. London: Bloomsbury, p. 16.

35 Barthes, R., 1967. *The Fashion System*. New York: Hill.

36 Wilkinson-Weber, C., 2013. *Fashioning Bollywood: The Making and Meaning of Hindi Film Costume*. Oxford: Berg, p. 115.

37 Dwyer, R., and D. Patel, 2002. *Cinema India: The Visual Culture of Hindi Film*. London: Reaktion Books, p. 88.

38 Sandhu, A., 2014, *ibid.*, p. 60.

39 Mathur, S., 2007. *India by Design: Colonial History and Cultural Display*. California and London: University of California Press; Mazzarella, W., 2003, *ibid*.

40 Menkes, S., *Vogue*, 3 October 2014. 'Rahul Mishra: Being Good and Doing Good': http://www.vogue.co.uk/news/2014/10/01/suzy-menkes---fashion-week-round-up

41 Brown, R., 2009. *Art for a Modern India, 1947–1980*. Durham, N.C.: Duke University, p. 159.

Glossary

achkan A knee-length coat for men.

anarkali A longer form of the *kurta* with panels making up the skirt and often a front flap that ties at the chest.

angrakha A coat with long sleeves and full skirt.

bandhgala Nehru (closed-collar) jacket.

chanderi A fine silk handwoven in and around the town of Chanderi in Madhya Pradesh, Central India.

charkha Spinning-wheel closely associated with the symbolism of the Swadeshi movement: a spinning-wheel sits at the heart of the Indian flag which must be made from handspun and handwoven *khadi*.

chikankari Embroidery associated with Lucknow in North India. Usually white thread on semi-sheer white fabric, the techniques include shadow work, where satin stitch is undertaken on the wrong side of the fabric and outlined with tiny running stitches on the right side, and *jail*, a form of openwork embroidery combined with other techniques such as French knots.

choli A cropped fitted blouse. Variations include long, short or sleeveless *cholis*. They may also be backless, featuring details such as lacing and tassels.

churidar Trousers made with extra fabric at the bottom. They fit tightly at the ankles and lower calves, resulting in dense folds of gathered fabric known as *chunni(s)*.

desi Derived from the ancient Sanskrit (*deśá* or *deshi*) which means 'country'. In the context of Indian popular culture, it is often used to describe the uniquely 'Indian' qualities of something.

dhoti An unstitched garment worn by men on the lower body. The practice of draping it between the legs and tucking the end into the waistband at the back results in a divided garment that functions similarly to trousers. It is usually worn with a *kurta*.

dupatta Scarf or stole worn with the *salwar kameez*, it may be draped over the head or is often worn in a cowl drape around the neck and shoulders.

gota patti Form of embroidery using appliquéd gold ribbon from Rajasthan in northern India.

ikat A highly skilled and precise dyeing technique used to pattern textiles. Uses a resist-dyeing process on the warp or weft fibres, or in the rare and costly 'double *ikat*', both warp and weft are resist dyed with intricate patterns only visible once woven on the loom.

kalire Umbrella-shaped ornaments that are hung from a bride's bangles.

kameez Long shirt or tunic.

khadi Handspun and handwoven cloth iconic to the freedom movement led by Mahatma Gandhi. Wearing Indian-spun and -woven *khadi* was a core aspect to the Swadeshi movement and was especially important when the British flooded the Indian market with imported cloth from Manchester.

kurta A loose tunic worn by men and women.

kurti A shorter version of the *kurta* worn by both sexes.

lehenga A full-panelled skirt. In north India it is often heavily embroidered and popular for weddings.

mehendi Henna.

mulmul A fine soft muslin.

Nivi style A style of sari draping where the end of the sari, the *pallu*, is draped across the torso and over the left shoulder towards the back.

pallu The end of the sari that is draped over the shoulder or sometimes wrapped around the head.

resham Soft, untwisted raw silk thread used in embroidery.

salwar Loose trousers with a drawstring waist.

salwar kameez (also spelt *shalwar kameez*) A combination of *salwar* (loose trousers) and *kameez* (a long tunic). It can be hugely varied according to cut, fabric and ornamentation. In popular terms it is often referred to simply as a 'suit'.

sari An unstitched length of fabric, six or nine yards in length, with a border, body and *pallu* (end piece) that determine how it will look when worn.

sari-gown In appearance, it is draped and pleated like a sari, but these elements are pre-stitched and it is put on like a dress with the aid of hooks or zippers to fasten it.

sherwani A long coat similar to the *achkan*, but made from heavier fabric and lined. Historically associated with the Indian aristocracy, it is now popular for weddings and formal functions.

Swadeshi Literally means 'things of one's own country'. The Swadeshi movement brought together the political aim of freedom from colonial rule and the goal of economic sovereignty through the production and consumption of Indian-made goods.

zardosi Embroidery using metal thread, often heavy and incorporating sequins, beads and other elements.

zari Gold thread.

Further Reading

Appadurai, A., 1996. *Modernity at Large: Cultural Dimensions in Globalization.* Minnesota: University of Minnesota Press.

Arnold, R., 2009. *Fashion: a Very Short Introduction.* Oxford: Oxford University Press.

Barthes, R., 1967. *The Fashion System.* New York: Hill.

Bayly, C. A., 1986. 'The Origins of *Swadeshi* (home industry): Cloth and Indian Society, 1700–1930' in A. Appadurai (ed.) *The Social Life of Things: Commodities in Cultural Perspective.* Cambridge: Cambridge University Press.

Boulanger, C., 1997. *Saris: an Illustrated Guide to the Indian Art of Draping.* Delhi: Shakti Press International.

Bourdieu, P., 1984. *Distinction: a Social Critique of the Judgment of Taste.* London: Routledge and Kegan Paul.

Breward, C., 2003. *Fashion.* Oxford: Oxford University Press.

Brosius, C., 2010. *India's Middle Class: Urban Forms of Leisure, Consumption and Prosperity.* London: Routledge.

Brubaker, R., and F. Cooper, 2000. 'Beyond "Identity"', *Theory and Society* 29 (1): 1–47.

Chapman, J., 2005. *Emotionally Durable Design: Objects, Experiences and Empathy.* London: Earthscan.

Crane, D., 1997. 'Globalization, Organizational Size, and Innovation in the French Luxury Fashion Industry. Production of Culture Theory Revisited', *POETICS* 24(6): 393–414.

Crill, R., 1999. *Indian Embroidery.* London: Victoria and Albert Museum.

Dwyer, R. and D. Patel, 2002. *Cinema India: The Visual Culture of Hindi Film.* London: Reaktion Books.

Eicher, J. (ed.), 1995. *Dress and Ethnicity: Change Across Space and Time.* Oxford: Berg.

Entwistle, J., 2009. *The Aesthetic Economy of Fashion.* Oxford: Berg.

Gandhi, M. K., 1989 (1927). *An Autobiography or Stories of my Experiments with Truth.* Ahmedabad: Navajivan Publishing House.

Geczy, A., 2013. *Fashion and Orientalism: Dress, Textiles and Culture from the 17th to the 21st Century.* London: Bloomsbury.

Jansen, M. A., 2012. 'Notions of Tradition and Modernity in the Construction of National Fashion Identities'. http://www.inter-disciplinary.net/critical-issues/wp-content/uploads/2013/09/AJansen_wpaper-fash5.pdf. Accessed May 2015.

Jumabhoy, Z., 2010. *The Empire Strikes Back: Indian Art Today.* London: Jonathan Cape.

Kapur Chishti, R. Singh, M. and R. Kelkar, 2010. *Saris of India: Tradition and Beyond.* Delhi: Roli Books.

Kapur, G., 2000. *When was Modernism: Essays on Contemporary Cultural Practice in India.* Delhi: Tulika Books.

Karlekar, M., 2005. *Re-visioning the Past: Early Photography in Bengal 1875–1915.* Delhi and Oxford: Oxford University Press.

Khaire, M., 2011. 'Context, Agency, and Identity: The Indian Fashion Industry and Traditional Indian Crafts.' *Business History Review*, 85(2).

Khosla, R. and A. Johnston, 1996. *Rohit Khosla: Vanguard.* Mumbai: India Book House.

Mathur, S., 2007. *India by Design: Colonial History and Cultural Display.* California and London: University of California Press.

Mazzarella, W., 2003. *Shoveling Smoke: Advertising and Globalization in Contemporary India.* Durham, N.C. and London: Duke University Press.

Niessen, S., Leshkowich, A. M. and C. Jones (eds), 2003. *Re-orienting Fashion: the Globalization of Asian Dress.* Oxford: Berg.

Patel, D., 2014. *India: Contemporary Design: Fashion, Graphics, Interiors.* Delhi: Roli Books.

Pinney, C., 1999. 'On Living in the Kal(i)yug: Notes from Nagda, Madhya Pradesh', *Contributions to Indian Sociology*, 33 (1–2): 77–106.

Polhemus, T., and L. Procter, 1978. *Fashion and Anti-fashion: an Anthropology of Clothing and Adornment.* London: Thames & Hudson.

Radhakrishnan, S., 2011. *Appropriately Indian: Gender and Culture in a New Transnational Class.* Durham, N.C. and London: Duke University Press.

Ramaswamy, S., 2009. *The Goddess and the Nation: Mapping Mother India.* Durham, N.C: Duke University Press.

Rodricks, W., 2012. *Moda Goa.* Noida: HarperCollins Publisher India Ltd.

Rodricks, W., 2012. *The Green Room.* Delhi: Rupa Publications.

Sandhu, A., 2014. *Indian Fashion: Tradition, Innovation, Style.* London: Bloomsbury.

Sengupta, H., 2009. *Ramp Up: The Business of Indian Fashion.* Delhi: Pearson.

Sinha, G., Jani, A. and S. Khosla, 2012. *India Fantastique.* London: Thames & Hudson.

Trivedi, L., 2007. *Clothing Gandhi's Nation.* Indianapolis: Indiana University Press.

Vasudev, S., 2012. *Powder Room: The Untold Story of Indian Fashion.* Delhi: Ebury Press.

Wilkinson-Weber, C., 2013. *Fashioning Bollywood: The Making and Meaning of Hindi Film Costume.* Oxford: Berg.

Online articles
Payal and Priyankha, 31 December 2013. 'Rewind 2013', *High Heel Confidential*: http://www.highheelconfidential.com/?s=it%20sure%20as%20hell%20was%20memorable

Vasudev, S., 17 August 2013. 'Profile: Anamika Khanna', *LiveMint*: http://www.livemint.com/Leisure/tTxH0WTDdEF18wKmfPXKIM/Profile--Anamika-Khanna.html

Vasudev, S., 16 October 2010. 'Free-to-Wear-Anything Country'. *The Indian Express*: http://archive.indianexpress.com/news/freetowearanything-country/698459/

Sujata Assomull Sippy. 10 August 2012. 'Runway Review: Anamika Khanna at Couture Week'. *Fashion Focus. Vogue India*: http://www.vogue.in/content/runway-review-anamika-khanna-couture-week

Sinha, C., 22 October 2012. 'Kallol Datta's Inspiration'. *Crossing Over – Fragments from a Journey*: http://chinkisinha.blogspot.co.uk/2012/10/kallol-dattas-inspiration.html

Editor's blog, 16 May 2011. 'Abu-Sandeep Style Directors for GVK Wedding in Hyderabad.' *Wedding Sutra*: http://weddingsutra.com/blog/index.php/2011/05/16/abu-jani-and-sandeep-khosla-style-directors-for-the-gvk-wedding

Lakshmi, R., 26 December 2008. 'From Low Art to High Fashion in India.' *Washington Post*: www.washingtonpost.com/wp-dyn/content/article/2008/12/25/AR2008122500909.html